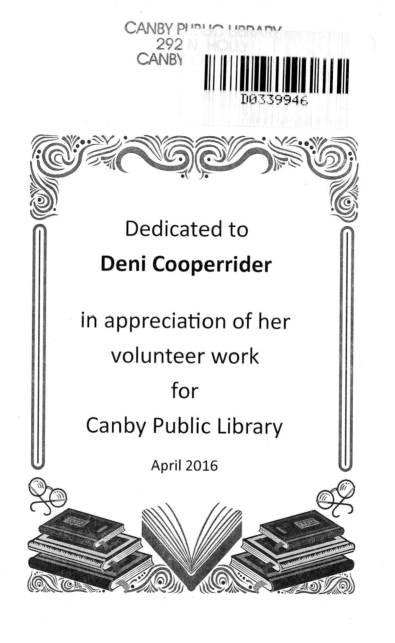

Dedicated to

Deni Cooperrider

in appreciation of her

volunteer work

for

Canby Public Library

April 2016

TED Books

The Boiling River

Adventure and Discovery in the Amazon

ANDRÉS RUZO

TED Books
Simon & Schuster

New York   London   Toronto   Sydney   New Delhi

TEDBooks

Simon & Schuster, Inc.
1230 Avenue of the Americas
New York, NY 10020

First TED Books hardcover edition February 2016

TED BOOKS and colophon are registered
trademarks of TED Conferences, LLC

SIMON & SCHUSTER and colophon are registered trademarks
of Simon & Schuster, Inc.

For information about special discounts for bulk purchases,
please contact Simon & Schuster
Special Sales at 1-866-506-1949 or
business@simonandschuster.com.

For information on licensing the TED Talk
that accompanies this book, or other content
partnerships with TED, please contact
TEDBooks@TED.com.

Jacket and interior design by: MGMT. design
Cover photo ©Aliaksandr Kazantsau / Stockfresh
(Not actual image of Boiling River)

Manufactured in the United States of America

10 9 8 7 6 5 4 3 2 1

Library of Congress Cataloging-in-Publication Data is available.

ISBN 978-1-5011-1947-7

ISBN 978-1-5011-1948-4 (ebook)

To my greatest discovery:
my wife and field partner, Sofía

CONTENTS

The Boiling River

1 Revelations in the Dark

I am standing on a rock in the middle of a river. Nighttime in the jungle pours around me. Instinctively, I reach up and turn off my headlamp. The blackness is complete now and I pause, waiting. I had missed the darkness. I breathe in. The air is thick and abnormally hot, even for the Amazon. As my eyes adjust to the dark, the outline of the jungle slowly distinguishes itself from the night: blacks, grays, dark blues, even silvery whites. It's amazing what we miss when the lights are on. The moon is hardly a sliver, and innumerable stars dominate the sky above, illuminating the vast jungle and bathing each leaf and rock with their soft light. All around me, vapors rise like ghosts in the starlight. Some are thin streams of mist; others are clouds so large that their billowing appears to be in slow motion.

I lie down on the rock and am still, watching the steam rise into the night. When a cool breeze blows, the mists thicken and roll, forming pale gray-blue eddies against the sky. The rock beneath my body glows dimly white in the faint light. Where my back and legs touch the rock's surface, I'm sweating lightly. A torrent of water, hot enough to kill me, wider than a two-lane road, surges past my rock, emitting a roar that drowns out the jungle's nighttime chorus. My senses are sharp and every movement is keenly deliberate.

I'm in the heart of the Peruvian Amazon. The other members of my team are in bed in the tiny community nearby, but there is no way I can sleep—not with what is before me here. My heart is beating hard, but I feel a complete calm. My eyes follow the river's vapors as they rise and melt into the firmament. The Milky Way flows across the sky like a reflection of the river below. The Inca referred to the Milky Way as the Celestial River, a path to another world, a place inhabited by spirits. So the vapors join two great rivers here. It's clear why the people who live here regard this jungle as a place of such spiritual power. The shaman's words echo in my head: "The river shows us what we need to see."

This is becoming one of the greatest adventures of my life. This will be the story I tell my children and grandchildren—and every action I make in this moment adds a new piece of the story. Every passing second now seems to hold a greater significance. Burning-hot water splashes on my right arm. I sit up, pulling my arm to my chest, no longer lost in thought. I recall my professor's words from volcanology field school: "The people who die on volcanoes are the inexperienced who are ignorant of the dangers and the experts who have forgotten they are dangerous."

I stand, make sure I have a firm footing, and jump back onto the nearest shore. As I look back at the Boiling River I can't suppress an excited whisper: "This place exists. This place actually exists." I remember the shaman saying the river has called me here for a purpose, and I can feel a greater mission about to take place. I won't get much sleep tonight.

The vapors dance in the starlight as I make my way back

to my hut, my mind filled with thoughts of the river, the dark jungle surrounding it, and the story that remains to be written. It's a story that began with a legend heard in childhood—a story of exploration and discovery, driven by a need to understand what initially appeared unbelievable. It's a story where modern science and traditional worldviews collide—not violently but respectfully—united in their sense of awe for the natural world.

At a time when everything seems mapped, measured, and understood, this river challenges what we *think* we know. It has forced me to question the line between known and unknown, ancient and modern, scientific and spiritual. It is a reminder that there are still great wonders to be discovered. We find them not just in the black void of the unknown but in the white noise of everyday life—in the things we barely notice, the things we almost forget, even in a detail of a story.

2 My Grandfather's Legend

The sound of hot water trickling into a teacup fills the cool air of the kitchen. I peer out the window at the Andean foothills that intrude into Lima's gray winter sky. Winter in Lima always has a certain stillness to it, and this August is no exception. I am twelve years old, sitting in the kitchen of my aunt's house, anxiously waiting for my grandfather to arrive.

While I stare at the clock impatiently, Dioni, my aunt's cook, stands at the sink, peeling fat Peruvian carrots. She is like a grandmother to me. "It is so good you came to visit," she says without lifting her eyes from her work. Dioni speaks Spanish with a strong Quechua accent. Quechua, the language of the Inca, is spoken in a deliberate, closed-mouth fashion—a result, it is said, of developing in the cold of the high Andes. Dioni's voice reminds me that, more than four hundred years after the Spanish conquest, the language of the Inca is still very much alive.

She continues, "Your aunt said your dad and his brothers took you up to Marcahuasi for a week! It's too high up, and you are too young!"

I sit on a bar stool at the end of the kitchen island and prepare my *mate de coca*, infusing the dusty green leaves in the hot water until it turns pale gold.

"Did you bring the leaves from Marcahuasi?" Dioni asks. I

nod. "Those are the real coca leaves, from the mountains—they taste much better than what we get at the supermarket."

I take my first sip and savor the earthy, herbal flavor. Just last week, on the cold Marcahuasi Plateau, I got debilitating altitude sickness. Drinking *mate de coca* was the only thing that made me feel better.

At last my grandfather walks through the door with outstretched arms. I run over to give him a hug, then laugh as he makes faces at me. Some people wear their hearts on their sleeves; he wears his on his face.

My aunt Lydia is with him. "Can I get you anything?" she asks my grandfather. "We have tea." His head shakes. "Coffee?" It shakes again. "Inca Kola? Juice? Water?" Finally: "Pisco?"

Now my grandfather's body straightens and a sly grin creeps across his face. "*Bueeeeeeno*, if you are offering it . . ."

She brings a fine silver tray bearing a neatly folded cloth napkin, a freshly opened bottle of excellent pisco with the cork just slightly reinserted into the bottle, and a crystal tulip-shaped flute. He pours and we toast, he with his pisco, me with my mate.

He begins to expound on the Marcahuasi trip and all the ways he would have done things better, smarter, and more efficiently had *he* been there. My attention drifts, and his voice recedes into the background.

Whack! A swift rap on the head with a rolled-up magazine gets my attention. "*Guanaco!* Listen! I'm telling you something important!" he scolds, making me scowl. To my surprise, his impatient expression softens into a proud smile.

"Your face is as animated as mine!" he says. "I'm glad my genes have not been lost on you." I'm still scowling.

"Okay, *cangrejo*, let me tell you a story to cheer you up."

I perk up in anticipation. I love my grandfather's stories.

"This is a story about adventure. A story of the Spanish conquest of Peru, the curse of the Inca, and a lost city hidden deep in the Amazon—made entirely of gold." I gaze at him, spellbound, as he takes another sip of pisco. "This is the legend of Paititi."

"Paititi?"

"Don't let anyone tell you the conquest was for God," my grandfather continues. "Sure, the conquistadors brought along a few monks, but what they really wanted was gold and glory." Cross-legged on the floor, I sit perfectly still as my grandfather begins.

In 1532, Francisco Pizarro and his men landed in Peru, at the northern border of the Inca Empire. The Inca were engaged in a violent civil war and had spies everywhere. From the moment they landed, the Spanish were being secretly watched by the Inca—their movements and habits tracked and reported. The Inca knew the conquistadores were not gods, but there was one thing in particular that they could not comprehend—their obsession with gold. The Inca told stories of Spaniards entering villages with no greeting other than: Where is the gold? and terrorizing the villagers until they obtained it. Their lust for gold was so insatiable that many Inca believed the Spaniards needed to eat gold to survive. To the Inca, who saw gold as divinity made manifest, this rapacity was confusing.

Atahualpa, emperor of the Inca, wondered how to deal with

these foreigners who were harassing his subjects. An advisor told him to capture them and burn them alive. But Atahualpa was more curious than afraid. What threat did 170 thieving white men pose? He, Atahualpa, was lord over millions. He commanded an army more than 250,000 strong. He was the most powerful god-man on earth, son of the sun, master of the magic of the winds.

Atahualpa sent emissaries to invite the foreigners to Cajamarca to meet with him. The conquistadors accepted. They then ambushed Atahualpa during what was meant to be a peaceful meeting. The Spaniards—vastly outnumbered but better armed—devastated the Inca.

Atahualpa, now a prisoner, glared defiantly into the eyes of his captors. None could meet his gaze, which they said was like looking into the sun. He walked ceremoniously to the nearest wall, reached his hand up as high as it could go, and drew a line. He summoned an attendant who leaned in as Atahualpa whispered into his ear. The attendant stood and told the Spanish, "The emperor says that he will fill this room to this line, once with gold and twice again with silver, if you spare his life and let him go."

The Spaniards spoke among themselves. That much gold and silver would make them wealthier than they had dreamed. They agreed to the terms. Atahualpa ensured that they swore their oath to their own god, the one who had delivered Atahualpa into their power.

For the next two months, the conquistadors watched as gold, silver, and precious stones poured in from across the empire to satisfy Atahualpa's ransom. Finally Atahualpa had completed his part of the deal. He would walk out, humbled but alive.

More months passed. Atahualpa's captors had not killed him, and he was kept in relative comfort, but he was still a prisoner. "They will not break their oath to their own god," he told himself.

One night, an attendant came to Atahualpa and whispered to him, "I overheard the Spaniards saying that you are too dangerous to keep alive. Your captors will break their oath and come for you tomorrow." A Spanish guard passed by and demanded to know what the attendant was doing. "I am only giving the emperor fresh coca leaves for his morning tea," he said, handing Atahualpa a small cloth bag with fresh leaves. The guard saw the leaves and sent the attendant on his way. Atahualpa prepared for morning."

I drink the last of my coca leaf tea, imagining Atahualpa as he realized he had been betrayed.

"The next day," my grandfather continues, "Atahualpa awoke to learn that he would be taken to trial under armed escort."

Atahualpa had no weapon with which to defend himself. As his captors came closer Atahualpa reached into the cloth bag. He brought out three leaves in his two hands and began to shout, "'By these leaves I damn you, white men! Mama Coca, remember their wickedness! Plague their nations and avenge me!" He threw the leaves at the Spaniards, sealing the curse that the coca leaves would bring upon them.

Atahualpa was executed but the Inca fought on. It took another forty years for the Spaniards to complete their conquest. The struggle finally ended in 1572, when Túpac Amaru, Lord of Serpents and last emperor of the Inca, was hung in the main plaza of Cusco before fifteen thousand of his subjects.

The Inca were conquered, and their sacred gold—a symbol of life itself—was melted down to satisfy their conquerors.

New waves of would-be conquistadors arrived, eager to follow in the footsteps of Cortés and Pizarro. When they asked the Inca where they could find another civilization to conquer, the Inca told them, "To the east, beyond the Andes, lies the land of the plant. There you will find Paititi—a vast city made entirely of gold."

The Spaniards launched expeditions into the Amazon, and the Inca looked on with stoic faces, knowing they were about to get the thing they wanted most—vengeance.

The few Spanish who returned from the Amazon told stories of sheer terror. They met Inca who had fled the conquest, who forced the Spaniards to drink molten gold to finally quench their gold lust. They also met Amazonians: powerful shamans who commanded the jungle itself to attack, and fierce warriors whose poison arrows killed men in seconds.

"They had entered a place where the trees grew so tall they blotted out the sun," my grandfather whispers. "They marched in perpetual darkness. Mosquitos and biting flies left them drained of blood. The jungle drove them mad with green monotony, taunted them with the sounds of game they never saw and pools of freshwater full of disease. Starvation, dehydration, and madness were their only companions. They told of snakes that swallowed men whole, spiders that ate birds—even of a river that boiled."

"They never found Paititi, and the jungle once thought to contain Eden itself proved to be a living hell."

My grandfather exhales and sits back to enjoy his pisco. I look on, unable to utter a word, my imagination running wild with thoughts of the jungle, the mysterious Paititi, and images of fierce shamans, giant snakes, and a steaming, bubbling river. I barely notice my aunt walking in.

She purses her lips as she evaluates my grandfather. "I can see you have had enough," she says, taking up the now half-empty bottle and tray.

My grandfather laughs as my aunt walks out the door. He turns to me, still smiling, and says, "*Aye, papachito*, the world is a big place. They are still looking for Paititi, by that and by many other names. But remember: the jungle keeps her secrets well, and she is not afraid to keep those who come after them."

3 Stupid Questions

"A boiling river?" scoffs the senior geologist. His suit is expensive, his hair is gray and precisely combed, and his brow is wrinkled. His is the face of modern Peru—a blend of indigenous and European. He speaks with the confidence and authority earned over decades of exploration in Peru's wild places. His large corporate office speaks of his success: *huacos* (artifacts), rock samples, and cultural pieces from all over Peru sit between leather-bound books on shelves made of dark, rich Amazonian wood. I could not help but think I was in the gentleman's study of a twenty-first-century conquistador, displaying the tokens of his conquests.

"Yes," I reply, "the legend mentioned 'a river that boiled' in the heart of the Peruvian Amazon. I know stories get exaggerated, but I'm still curious to see if there is any truth to it."

He casts me a disdainful look from across his imposing desk.

It is May 2011, and I am a twenty-four-year-old PhD student from Southern Methodist University (SMU) in Dallas. My field is geophysics, specializing in geothermal studies. I'm here in Lima to start my doctoral fieldwork. My goal—the focus of my research—is to create Peru's first detailed geothermal map, also called a "heat flow map." This type of map quantifies the thermal energy flowing through the earth's crust to its surface, and is useful in three main ways. First, geothermal maps identify areas of renewable geothermal energy potential. Second, they help make the oil and gas industry "greener" by providing information that makes exploration and drilling more precise (this means fewer needlessly drilled wells). Finally, geothermal maps are essential tools for better understanding tectonics, volcanology, seismology, and other fields within the geosciences.

But geothermal maps are notoriously difficult to make. At each "heat flow site" you need precise temperature data and rock samples from deep in the earth. Geothermal researchers often find that kilometers of rock separate us from the measurements or samples we need. Plus, drilling a new well is expensive and can often have negative environmental impacts. Barriers like these are why I've started meeting with oil, gas, and mining companies; where possible, I'm hoping to repurpose existing oil, gas, and mining wells for my geothermal studies, using those holes to get my deep-earth temperature data without drilling any new wells.

The corporate geologist likes that idea but is noticeably unimpressed by the question about my grandfather's legend.

"Andrés, you're a bright kid," he says now. "Your mapping research is interesting, and using existing infrastructure is a good idea, very innovative. So why this random fascination with an old legend? I don't know of any Amazonian boiling rivers. Peru has all sorts of geothermal features but a boiling river in the jungle is hard to believe. You should know that—you're the one getting the PhD."

I had completely forgotten about the legend until last year, when I visited colleagues at INGEMMET (the Peruvian government's Institute of Geology, Mining, and Metallurgy). They had prepared a map of Peru's known geothermal features—things like hot springs and fumaroles. Looking at it awakened the dormant memory of my grandfather's legend, and the image of a "river that boiled."

When I asked my colleagues, they reported that they had encountered geothermal features in the jungle, but nothing as large as a boiling river. The consensus was that such a thing was unlikely and probably just an exaggerated tale. My grandfather was by now suffering from dementia and couldn't help me find the source of the story. So I asked other geologists, from energy and mining companies, universities, and government institutions, if they had heard of a "boiling river" in the Amazon. They always answered no—but none as insistently as this senior geologist.

"Tell me, what is needed to generate a boiling river? Significant water flow and a tremendous source of heat. Boiling rivers do exist in the world, but every one I have ever heard of is associated with an active volcanic or magmatic system—which we don't have in the Amazon. You said you hope this geothermal map will help us understand why most of Peru's volcanism 'turned off' some two million years ago. You of all people should know how unlikely it is that this legend has any truth to it.

"Again, you're a bright kid. But as a friendly recommendation: I'd stop asking stupid questions. It makes you look bad."

I walk out of the office building with as much dignity as I can muster and hail a taxi.

I must have sounded so naive, I think. *The old geologist is right: if I want to be a well-respected scientist, I can't go around asking stupid questions. I can't find the legend in any written accounts, the science makes it unlikely, the experts have never heard of it— it's time to lay this thing to rest. Sometimes a story is just a story.*

4 A Detail in a Story

It's early June 2011. I've been in Lima with my wife, Sofía, for two weeks, preparing for the next few months of fieldwork in the oilfields of the Talara Desert in northwestern Peru, where we'll be temperature logging abandoned oil wells for the Geothermal Map of Peru. We've been staying at my uncle Eo and aunt Guida's house, and this evening they're having a small farewell dinner for us. I find myself sitting next to Guida.

"Andrés, *querido!*" she says, her Spanish marked by her native Brazilian accent. "It feels like you just got here!" I assure her that we will be back in Lima in a few months.

"You've been at your research for two years now," Guida says. "Have you found anything that has really surprised you?"

I take a sip of pisco. The professional answer would be something about mapping Peru's geothermal energy potential. But last week's meeting with the old geologist had been on my mind. Maybe it was the pisco, or my still-injured pride, but something made me open up to her about my attempts to find the truth about my grandfather's story, and the stupid questions I've been asking eminent scientists.

"It's probably just a story," I conclude. "But I'm still curious about it."

Guida looks puzzled. Slowly, she says, "Andrés, but there *is* a large thermal river in the jungle. I've been there. I swam in it!"

I know Guida to be a joker. "C'mon, *tía*," I say, laughing.

"It's true," she says, her face serious.

My uncle Eo, sitting on Guida's other side, chimes in: "She's not kidding! You can only swim in it after a very heavy rain, and then in certain parts, where it's cooler."

I'm stunned. Eo is a well-known psychoanalyst. He speaks precisely, and he wouldn't embellish for the sake of a story.

"You're serious?" I ask firmly.

"It's a sacred place, protected by a powerful shaman," Guida says.

"Your aunt is friends with his wife, who is a nurse," Eo continues.

Guida nods. "They have a healing center there called Mayantuyacu, and the river flows right in front of it. As wide as a two-lane road, and fast!"

I know my aunt used to do social and conservation work with native communities in the Amazon. Still, I'm skeptical. I grab my iPhone and search for "Mayantuyacu" online. There are no results. This surprises Guida and Eo, who insist that foreign patients regularly visit the medicinal center. They were invited to visit by a friend who works with the Asháninka community there.

"Where is it?" I ask, pulling up Google Earth on my phone.

"In the jungle somewhere in the central Peruvian Amazon," Guida says. "It takes about four hours to get there from Pucallpa—you have to take a car, then a motorized canoe, and then walk."

I study the terrain on my phone, trying to zero in on

Mayantuyacu's most likely location based on my aunt's and uncle's descriptions, and my own geologic knowledge of where geothermal systems generally come to the surface. The resolution on the satellite imagery is very low, but I am able to make out what looks like a large oval landform some three by five miles across, and about thirty miles south of Pucallpa. It has a prominent rim, and a broad dome rising from its center.

"At the river," I ask, "is there any smell of sulfur—like rotten eggs?" It's hydrogen sulfide that gives many volcanic systems their characteristic stench.

"There is no sulfur smell," Guida says, looking at Eo, who nods in agreement.

"Do you remember how long the river flows for?" I urge them.

"I'm not sure how long it is," Eo replies, "but it flows very hot for at least two hundred yards. There are a number of curves, so it's difficult to guess the true scale, but it is a formidable sight."

I continue searching on my phone, hoping to find any leads about Mayantuyacu or its sacred river somewhere online. Still nothing turns up. Though I know how unlikely it is, the dim hope of stumbling across the river I once heard of in a story is intoxicating.

I'm ignoring the party. Guida puts her motherly hand on my arm and says, "Maybe Mr. Google is just having a bad night." I give her a weak smile, my disappointment clear.

"Don't worry," she says, "I'll get you Mayantuyacu's telephone number and e-mail. You can contact them tomorrow."

I reel my mind back to the present, but I'm impatient for the night to pass. I need to find out more.

The next day we rise early to catch the plane for our months-long stay in Talara. Before we leave I call the number my aunt gave me and leave a message. Phone lines in the jungle can be less than reliable, so I send an e-mail, too. When we land, I check my voice mail and e-mail. No response.

Over the next few months I repeatedly try calling and e-mailing Mayantuyacu, but I don't get a single response. My hope and excitement have turned into frustration.

I review the geologic literature for reports of a large thermal river anywhere near Pucallpa. I find nothing. There is no such river on Peruvian government maps. The only study I can find that even mentions a geothermal feature in the area is a 1965 United States Geological Survey (USGS) compilation of the hot springs of the world. This USGS work makes a vague reference to a "small, warm spring" on the Agua Caliente (Hot Water) Dome, the feature I had noticed on Google Earth.

The USGS's reference to the "small, warm spring" cites a 1945 study, but that earlier study doesn't mention any geothermal features. The 1945 study leads me to a 1939 study, from which I learn that the dome was the site of the first oil development in the Peruvian Amazon—but which also makes no mention of any hot springs. However, it leads me to the first and only geologic study on the Agua Caliente Dome, conducted prior to oil development—a 1933 report by Moran and Fyfe.

This Moran paper proves to be a dead end. I look everywhere but can't find a copy. I'll have to continue my search back in the United States.

Months pass, and our field season in the desert comes to an

end. It is now late October, and we're back at Eo and Guida's house for a last week in Lima before returning to Dallas.

"Have you heard from Mayantuyacu?" Guida asks.

"Nothing," I say. I open my laptop to search for Mayantuyacu yet again. "I keep checking online, hoping to find something, but—*oh wow!*"

Guida quickly leans in to see my screen. There it is: www.mayantuyacu.com.

"You've got to be kidding me!" I exclaim. "The shaman got a website!"

"*El Perú avanza.*" Guida laughs. Peru advances!

The website lists a phone number, an e-mail address, and a physical address in Pucallpa. I realize with disappointment that it's the same number and e-mail I've been trying to reach.

"Now you have an address," Guida says hopefully, as she sits down next to me on the couch. "Listen, Andrés—I have worked with indigenous peoples in many parts of the Amazon. The people there have an interesting relationship with the modern world. The Amazonians resisted the Inca, and for the most part resisted the Spanish—until they were rounded up and treated worse than animals. Honestly, I'm not surprised that they never responded. I'm sure they received and read all your e-mails and listened to your voice mails. But what did you say? '*Hola,* my name is Andrés Ruzo, I am a geologist studying geothermal energy, I have a grant from *National Geographic,* I have been working in Talara, I want to study your site . . .'"

As I hear this aloud, my foolishness is clear. Guida goes on, in a softer voice: "I know why you became a geologist. I know why you do what you do and why you study geothermal energy. I know you are a good kid who is honest, who can be trusted, who would never put their sacred place in danger—but *they* don't know that. Think of all the big developments in the Amazon. Geologists have been on the front lines of 'progress' in the region since oil, gas, and mining development began. Remember that Mayantuyacu is a sacred site, and put that in the context of historical abuses of the Amazonians . . . well, is it any wonder that they haven't returned your phone calls?"

"So what should I do?" I ask, exasperation creeping into my voice.

Firmly, Guida says, "We need to go into the jungle."

5 Hidden in Plain Sight

A few isolated peaks emerge through the low clouds like brown islands in a sea of white. The peaks become more frequent, until they come together to form long chains—a great wall that keeps out the coastal clouds. We are flying over the Andes, the longest continental mountain range on earth.

From up here I can read the ridges and landforms. The mountains tell of tectonic forces—invisible hands that created alpine lakes and fertile valleys. These valleys were the breadbasket of the Inca and are still farmed by their descendants. Colossal geologic folds shape the land, bringing precious materials close enough to the surface for humans to mine.

My aunt Guida is asleep in the seat next to me. "They will never get back to you over e-mails or phone calls," she had told me last night in Lima. "It's easy to be tricked over the phone or by e-mail, but when someone is looking at you in the eye and you spend time with them, you can see their true colors pretty quickly. You need to meet them in person. I'll take you there."

There were plenty of reasons not to go. I leave for Dallas in less than a week. I'm on a grad-student budget. We don't even know if the shaman will be there—and even if he is, will he want to talk to me?

But if there is a boiling river out there, I'm convinced my best chance to see it is to buy a plane ticket right away, show up unannounced at the address in Pucallpa from the website, and ask permission to visit Mayantuyacu and their sacred river, four hours into the jungle.

Gradually the Andes become lower and greener. The plane descends through the clouds, and when we reemerge the world has transformed. Greens have replaced browns, trees have replaced rocks, and Amazonia stretches before us in every direction.

It's November, peak wet season. Engorged rivers and streams rush through the jungle, and rays of sunlight reflect off the inflated marshes. My eyes follow the flat, green jungle as it stretches to the horizon, my mind brimming over with questions. Where in this vast landscape could Mayantuyacu be hiding? Could this *really be* the river from my grandfather's legend? Does it actually boil?

On landing in the city of Pucallpa, we procure a ride. The driver of the weathered, rickety, three-wheeled motorcycle taxi is a round Amazonian man. He keeps his ear pressed to the latest smartphone—which looks more expensive than his taxi. We squeeze into the backseat.

As we make our bumpy way to the Mayantuyacu Office, Guida and I don't say much and I wonder if we're both thinking the same thing: *I hope the address is the same.* I try and push the thought away by looking out the window. This is my first time in the Amazon, and any travel fatigue I was feeling has now been driven out by excitement. Peru is often called three countries in one: coast, mountains, and jungle. Though Pucallpa's colors and landscape are clearly different from the coasts and mountains I know well, I am surprised by how familiar it feels.

Pucallpa is a large, modern city of the developing world—globalization decorated with the traditional. Modern buildings and installations, good roads, and a plethora of shopping centers all speak of progress. I watch many new, well-kept cars and motorcycles whiz past us. Our driver has been chattering nonstop on his phone since we left the airport. His radio plays Amazonian Cumbia, while the taxi's old plastic covering flaps beat noisily as the engine whines.

We putt our way through the city and into Pucallpa's suburbs. "Almost there," the taxi driver yells to us over his radio, still on the phone. We turn off the paved street and onto a reddish dirt road with occasional large, water-filled potholes.

"There it is!" Guida suddenly cries. The taxi comes to a sharp stop. I follow where Guida is pointing: a green wood-paneled building on the left. "All these years, it hasn't changed!"

We send the taxi driver off, and Guida knocks on the windowless, knobless door.

"Who is it?" comes a woman's apprehensive voice.

"*Hola!* This is Guida, an old friend of Sandra and Maestro Juan's. Are they home?"

The green door opens slowly to reveal a young Amazonian woman with light mahogany skin, dark upturned eyes, and jet-black hair. She introduces herself and tells us that Sandra and Maestro are away. "But we can call them," she offers. We nod excitedly and she opens the door wide, ushering us through a dim, narrow wooden hallway and into a large office. As Guida and the woman make the phone call, I take in the room.

Everything has been organized with care, from the trinkets

on the shelves to the pictures on the walls, each depicting happy faces with broad white grins and dark, piercing eyes. Intricate geometric patterns of Shipibo design also decorate pots, figures, and textiles. An Asháninka robe and headdress are displayed on a wall, surrounded by bows and arrows, seed necklaces, snail shells, tropical feathers, and thick dried vines.

Along with the traditional ornaments are signs of modern Peru: small Peruvian flags and large posters of the "Wonders of Peru." To my surprise, a framed poster of the Monument to Humanity, Marcahuasi's iconic human-faced monolith, hangs between those of Machu Picchu and the Nazca Lines. Marcahuasi—where I succumbed to altitude sickness as a boy and was comforted by *mate de coca*—is less well-known than the world-famous sites displayed on the wall. I was glad to see it there—my connection to that place runs deep.

My great-grandfather Daniel Ruzo devoted the latter part of his life to understanding Marcahuasi and is attributed with revealing it to the world. A philosopher and explorer by nature, he worked tirelessly to protect this mysterious Andean plateau, full of ruins and seemingly carved monoliths. Thanks to his photography and publications, the virtually unknown, unprotected site became a cherished national park, where tourism has become an economic lifeline for the local people.

Along with traditional honor and Peruvian pride, the decorations here tell a surprising third story. A golden Chinese money-frog sits next to a ceramic Indian elephant with American dollar bills tucked into its trunk. A large Mexican painting of the Virgin of Guadalupe watches over the room, flanked by postcards from Canada and a Spanish wineskin. Decorative images of Italy, Argentina, and Brazil hang next to Navajo ornaments from the American Southwest. I briefly wonder if Maestro Juan is a master of the Amazon or of amazon.com, but written notes and dedications identify the decorations as goodwill gifts from grateful tourists.

"You've got to be kidding me!" I laugh to myself. "Can all these people really have visited? This might be the best-known 'unknown' site in the world."

"Andrés!" Guida calls. "We were unable to reach Maestro— he is at Mayantuyacu, in the jungle, where there is no phone service. Normally they would not let us in without his approval, but we got ahold of Sandra, who recognized my voice and gave us the okay. Maestro is leaving Mayantuyacu today, and if we are lucky we can catch him before he leaves—but regardless, you'll see the river today."

I can barely contain my excitement. I hug her tightly, and she laughs. "*Aye querido*, we are not in the jungle yet! We still have a long journey ahead of us, and we had better get moving—I don't want you saying I brought you all this way just to show you the river in the dark!"

We spend the next two hours in another taxi, avoiding large, flooded potholes on a bumpy, reddish dirt road. I gaze at swaths of lush, impenetrable jungle interspersed with vast, verdant fields where a few cattle peacefully ruminate. The drive ends in the small town of Honoria, where we park in front of a large, grassy open space that slopes down to the mighty Pachitea River. At the bottom of the sloping bank, the chocolate-brown

Pachitea stretches over a thousand feet wide and flows with the power of a freight train.

I stretch my legs and watch the taxi speed away, red dust pluming behind. There is not a soul in sight, thanks to the midday sun beating down on the town. The only sign of life is music from a muffled radio in one of the houses. The buildings are made of wooden planks with corrugated metal roofs. Many are built on stilts to protect them from flooding.

"The Mayantuyacu guides are probably still coming out of the jungle. Let's get something to eat while we wait. That's the town restaurant over there," Guida says, pointing to a one-story, weathered, turquoise building built into the riverbank on tall stilts.

As we walk onto its long, covered terrace, the sound of our feet on the heavy wooden floorboards alerts the owner of our presence. A little old Amazonian woman appears, with an overjoyed expression, and a face wrinkled by a lifetime of smiling. Her Spanish is heavily marked with an Amazonian accent, and when she speaks it is with such tenderness that we feel immediately welcome.

"*Hola, hola!* Welcome to the jungle! What can I offer you today? We have Inca Kola, Coca-Cola, or water to drink. To eat, we have *huangana* with yucca and rice. We also have bagged chips."

"*Huangana?*" I ask.

"Jungle pig!"

We order bottled water and the dish of the day. As we settle in to our lunch, a man appears at the far end of the terrace. He wears knee-high plastic boots, stained with reddish mud, and his clothing is faded and frayed. He sits down at a table and stares furtively at us.

I give a friendly wave, hoping that he may have been sent by Mayantuyacu to pick us up. He doesn't respond but continues to stare. Guida and I try to ignore him. Before long another man appears on the terrace with a teenage boy. The three whisper to each other, and cast prying glances at our bags.

I smile and wave again. They don't return the gesture. I don't want to assume the worst, but experience working in rough areas has taught me to be cautious.

The old woman reappears with our food and we hungrily dig in. I remain attentive as I eat, giving them occasional stern looks to let the trio know I am watching them. Their glances grow more subtle.

As the old woman returns to clear our plates, Guida leans in and lowers her voice. "I am going to follow her and pay inside," she murmurs. "You can pay me back later. Just watch the bags."

Guida helps clear the dirty plates, then follows our hostess inside. Possible scenarios play out in my mind, I consider past courses of action that have kept me safe. Reaching into my left pocket, I feel the smooth beads of my rosary. I press the cross firmly between my fingers and place my hand back on the table. My right hand creeps under my shirt and unhooks the clasp around the handle of a hunting knife that I had hidden around my waist.

I am very glad Sofía is not here.

Suddenly, Guida bursts back onto the terrace with a stack of clear plastic cups and two large bottles of Inca Kola. "*Hola, chicos!*" she exclaims, addressing the trio with a wide smile. "You have not stopped looking at us since we got here. You should have just said hello! Here, have some soda, and I brought chocolates from Lima. We are going to Mayantuyacu to visit Maestro Juan and Sandra." Everyone on the terrace looks up at her, stunned. "Come on, there is chocolate and Inca Kola for everyone! I haven't been to Honoria in a long time—I want to hear all the gossip I've missed." The trio, quickly recovering from their shock, give sheepish smiles and accept the soda and chocolate.

Hearing the commotion, the old woman comes out and is thrilled. She rushes back inside and returns with seven more people—men, women, children, even a stray dog.

As more people arrive and the gathering turns into a genuine party, I laugh in amazement. Refastening the clasp that holds my knife, I think, *If only the conquest had been led by women, Peru would be a very different place today.*

As we finish we hear the sound of a motor. Looking upriver, we spot a *pekepeke*—a long, thin, wooden Amazonian riverboat that looks like an elongated canoe with a protruding prow. Its russet colors blend in with the Pachitea and the jungle—apart from the vessel's Peruvian flag, its red and white standing out against the natural colors. The boatman eases it onto the shore. Coming out of the kitchen, the old woman announces, "There are your guides. They will take you to Mayantuyacu."

6 Hopes and Hard Data

Pe-ke, pe-ke, pe-ke, pe-ke. Our motorized canoe emits a rhythmic mechanical sound as it beats against the Pachitea's current. Our captain, a little old Amazonian man, sits at the stern and mans the small engine. When he introduced himself to us, back in Honoria, Guida and I could hardly believe our ears.

"Francisco Pizarro? Like the conquistador?" I had asked.

"Yes, sir," he replied proudly.

For half an hour we ride along this watery highway through the jungle. Steep, muddy cliffs fifteen feet high border the banks. Thick green jungle erupts from the clifftops.

The trees are so tall, and the jungle so thick, that it is difficult to distinguish the topography above the ridge. In places, thatched-roof homesteads sit on lush lawns dotted with large trees and grazing cattle. These patches of domesticated jungle expose rolling hills and ravines.

"Isn't it incredible?" Guida says, beaming. "I love the jungle."

"It's beautiful." I nod. "But I just can't wait to see this thermal river. Honestly, I'm having trouble focusing on much else."

Guida laughs. "Try to enjoy the present a little more," she says. "The river will come soon enough."

We hear a shout from the front of the *pekepeke*, where our second guide, Brunswick, is standing. He is in his early thirties

Pushing off Honoria's muddy red banks, our *pekepeke* silently drifts with the mighty Pachitea River. The boat's motor breaks the silence as I enter the Amazon for the first time.

and is Maestro's apprentice. "Look over there!" he says, pointing some thirty feet ahead. "There is the mouth of the Boiling River where the hot and cold waters meet."

Finally, the river! My eyes scan the scene. A tributary to our right, wider than a two-lane road, is injecting a significant quantity of flow into the Pachitea. Where the two waters collide, a dusky olive-green plume of water curves into the Pachitea's chocolate brown. But I don't see even the slightest wisp of steam.

The prow enters the plume and Brunswick dips his hand into the green water, signaling to me to do the same.

I dip my hand into the cold brown water of the Pachitea. The moment we pass into the green plume, the water becomes warm. It gets warmer and warmer as we near the tributary, until finally we glide into its mouth. Here the water is significantly warmer, like hot bathwater—but nowhere near boiling.

I shouldn't feel disappointed, but my excitement has gotten the better of me. This "Warm River of the Amazon," is not the stuff of my dreams. The "Boiling River" has not lived up to its name. I let out a deep sigh.

Okay, no more speculation, no more expectations. I need to get to Mayantuyacu and let the river tell its own story. Focus on real quantifiable data, not hearsay.

Expertly navigating the *pekepeke*, Francisco steers the boat to shore, where steps carved into the cliff's reddish mud beckon us toward the next leg of our journey.

I turn on the path tracker on my GPS and slip it back into my backpack.

Disembarking, we climb to the top of the bank, where we see a thin, muddy trail entering the forest. Francisco pushes off and heads back to Honoria as Brunswick leads us into the jungle.

The trail is well trodden but uneven. Massive trees with imposing buttress roots shade us from the hot sun. Twisting vines with bizarre forms and textures snake through the foliage. Electric-colored flowers hang above us, so delicate and exotic that I find it hard to believe they are natural. As we hike up and down the undulating topography, hidden animals serenade us. Squadrons of mosquitos stalk us. Our liberally applied insect repelled forms a forcefield where a blanket of mosquitos hovers, just out of reach.

At the end of a large clearing, near the crest of a tall ridge, I notice a heavily eroded dirt road. I ask Brunswick about it.

"Loggers came through here many years ago in tractors and took away the big trees," he answers solemnly. "They were chased out, but the clearing remains."

Guida speaks in a pained tone. "Many years ago, I was doing social work with an indigenous group in the jungles far south of here. I was staying in a village on a large river, and though the area was supposedly protected, the locals were still having problems with illegal loggers. One night I couldn't sleep, so I took a walk to the river. When I got down to the bank, I heard strange noises. The full moon let me see clearly, though a part of me wishes I hadn't looked. From end to end, as far as I could see upstream and downstream, the river was full of massive *lupuna* trees. Men with long poles walked back and forth across the giant floating logs, guiding them

Deforestation in the Boiling River area is an ongoing tragedy. The large, valuable trees have been cut down and sold (most likely on illegal markets), and the remaining jungle has been torched to make way for agriculture.

downstream. It was clear why they were transporting the trunks at night.

"Each of those trees was easily hundreds of years old. This was exactly what I was helping the community to fight. I felt so hopeless, and I knelt down and wept.

"The next day, I relayed what I had seen. The villagers were all too familiar with this sort of scene. They described how the loggers would appear, cut down the big trees, then clear-cut

and burn swaths of land to form paths to roll or drag the trunks
to the nearest river, using tractors like the one that left the trail
we just saw."

A wave of anger washes over me. "That's terrible," I mutter.

"But the worst part came later," Guida continues. "We
discovered that most of those ancient trees were being used to
make plywood. Plywood! The *lupuna* is known as the Lady of
the Jungle. Their trunks can be more than three yards wide."

"They are thought to contain powerful spirits, and in some tribes it is considered a grave offense even to relieve oneself near one. And they are being used for *plywood*."

A depressed silence envelops our small group as we continue our journey through the jungle. My thoughts shift back to the Boiling River. If accounts of the river are true and not merely an exaggeration, there are three possible explanations: it's a volcanic/magmatic system, it's a nonvolcanic hydrothermal system where geothermal waters are quickly being brought to the surface from deep within the earth, or it's man-made.

This last possibility is disconcerting. What if the Boiling River is just the result of an oilfield accident—an improperly abandoned oil well, a frack job gone wrong, or oilfield waters improperly reinjected into the earth? I know of many cases, in Peru and abroad, where oilfield accidents have caused geothermal features—the most infamous being the Lusi mud volcano in East Java, which has displaced more than thirty thousand people. Accidents of this scale quickly take on significant financial and political importance, and as a result, Lusi's "true cause" remains a contentious issue. In the Talara Desert, I recently visited two tourist attractions with surprising backgrounds. The plan had been for two old oil wells— wells that were only producing warm, salty water—to be properly sealed and closed up by the oil companies. As the story goes, the locals saw potential in the pools of warm water and pressured the companies to keep the wells open. The oil companies gave in, and the wells were converted into bathing pools. Now unsuspecting tourists pay to relax in the "natural healing thermal waters" while rubbing the "rejuvenating" thermal muds on their faces.

I let out a long exhale as I realize that this horrible possibility might be the most likely explanation. We *are* near the oldest oilfield in the Peruvian Amazon—it's a well-studied area, and a large thermal river isn't exactly easy to miss. Furthermore, the river doesn't appear on the Peruvian government's geothermal feature map—though that 1965 report mentions a "small, warm spring" somewhere in this general area . . .

Maybe the river *was* a small, warm spring that accidentally became a boiling river. Maybe the legends came later—I've seen it happen in other parts of Peru. Maybe I'm walking into an oilfield cover-up. Accidents are bad for business, after all, and companies paying off government officials to ignore such "minor inconveniences" are hardly unheard of.

Frustrated, I shake my head to try to clear my mind. *I'm so sick of all these uncertainties,* I think. *Until I see real data I know nothing. I need a solid GPS location to determine exactly how close the river is to the nearest oilfield. I need precise temperature data to figure out how exaggerated these accounts are. Most important, I need to find that stupid 1933 Moran study—it's the only study done before this area was developed, and the only one left that could mention the river.*

I prepare myself to accept whatever outcome I find. Science is not about the story we want to hear—it's about the story the data tell us.

Just then Brunswick stops and points out a thick metal pipe, partially buried, running across the trail. "This oil pipeline once went from the oilfield to Pucallpa," he says. "They stopped using it years ago and most of it has been stolen now.

A sign at Mayantuyacu's property line tells clear-burners to keep out of their jungle. Curiously, the property line is determined by an old oil pipeline—a reminder that this area was the site of the first oil development in the Peruvian Amazon.

It marks our property boundary—from here to the river, we are in Mayantuyacu."

A large painted wooden sign reads: MAYANTUYACU—ZONA PROHIBIDA.

"Prohibited zone?" I turn to Brunswick. "Prohibited to whom?"

"Loggers, hunters, squatters. We are trying to do good work in Mayantuyacu—healing people and giving them traditional natural medicines. We get our knowledge from the plants and the grandparents." He pauses, looking up at a large, thick tree.

Brunswick gently places his hand on the tree trunk. "The spirits leave when the land is cleared."

Pointing to the sign, he adds: "*Mayantu* for the spirit of the jungle, and *Yacu* for the spirit of the water. Here we heal by working together with both spirits."

His words, spoken with profound respect, strike a chord in me. I resolve to keep my hypotheses to myself—even healthy scientific skepticism about the river could be misinterpreted as disrespect.

We reach the top of a second great ridge crowned by massive trees, guards of the surrounding jungle, and rest a moment, Guida and I taking deep ragged breaths. Our two-hour hike in the heat has taken the energy out of us.

"Almost there," Brunswick assures us.

As our gasps subside, I hear something in the distance.

"What's that sound?" I say. "It's like a low surge."

Brunswick raises his eyes to me and smiles. "The river."

7 The River

I stare at Brunswick and Guida in amazement. Fatigue forgotten, I rush to the edge of the hill to catch my first glimpse of the river, but I can't see anything through the foliage. Brunswick laughs and points down a steep path into the jungle below, urging me, "Go!"

I bolt down the dirt path, and the low surge grows louder. Through the trees I can make out a clearing where a few wooden buildings stand. Scattered wisps of white vapor rise above the treetops. I make my way around a building at the end of the path, and I am met with a stunning view. Turquoise waters rush past thin banks of ivory-colored rock. Giant trees rise to form walls of green flanking the river. Where the current crashes against the rocks there are patches of whitewater, indicating the force of the water's flow. I step onto the edge of a small cliff overlooking the river and scan the scene. My eyes follow the river bend as it disappears into the jungle ahead. The afternoon sun beats down on me. I am sweating. My heart pounds with excitement. Veils of white vapor drape the river's surface, playing in the breeze as they rise. *These waters must be very hot to be steaming at these air temperatures*, I think, breaking into a grin.

Upstream, a small, steaming creek bisects the Mayantuyacu community before cascading over the cliff into the river below. Beyond this waterfall, a sinewy form is visible through the mist—a strangely shaped tree, ten yards high, dark and haunting. If all the snakes in the jungle had entwined their bodies to form roots, a trunk, and branches, it wouldn't look too different from this tree. Its trunk is wrapped in thick, woody vines, and its branches spread like serpents from a Gorgon's head. It grows from the edge of the rocky cliff, its roots clinging to the rocks like great tentacles as it arches over the river.

I make my way to the twisted tree and spot a painted sign at its root that reads EL CAME RENACO. This attempt to mark the tree's significance seems superfluous. The Came Renaco's very shape—like something from a fairy tale—seems naturally significant: the home of a great spirit, perhaps, or the prison of a wicked one.

Below the mysterious tree I find steps hewn into the cliff, leading to the river's edge. As I descend, the river's roar grows louder. I feel the heat and humidity thicken around me as I step onto the limestone blocks that form a walkway next to the water's edge. Carefully, I lower myself onto the rocks and find them hot to the touch. The vapors roll and wrap around me. Between the river and the sun, it feels like I'm in a sauna inside a toaster oven.

I take off my backpack and unpack my thermometer, which I had protectively wrapped in clothes and plastic bags. I look at the river and say, "Moment of truth—let's see if you're really boiling. I begin the measurement. The thermometer's meter resembles an old Game Boy: a fat, clunky plastic box with a small display screen and a few of buttons. I screw a two-foot cable ending in a thick gray thermometer to the base of the

Mayantuyacu's iconic guardian tree, the Came Renaco. Locals believe its medicine is made more powerful by the Boiling River's vapors.

meter. Next, I calibrate the tool and slowly begin to dip the thermometer into the river. The current pulls it horizontal, but I continue carefully lowering until it's fully submerged. Holding my breath, I watch the readings equilibrate on the thermometer's screen.

The numbers settle, and I finally have my first temperature: 85.6°C, or around 186°F. At this elevation, water boils just under 100°C (212°F)—these waters are not boiling, but it's close enough to shock me. I definitely didn't expect this high a reading. Your average cup of coffee is served at around 54°C (130°F). Water becomes painful and dangerous around 47°C (around 117°F). Dipping my hand into the river would give me third-degree burns in less than half a second. Falling in could easily kill me.

After years of questions, doubts, literature reviews, dead ends, and frustrations, here at last is the Boiling River. The accounts may still be exaggerated, but clearly not by much.

I let the thermometer cool and repeat the measurement a few times. The temperatures consistently plot around 86°C (around 187°F). The temperatures, though impressive, are typical of many volcanic and nonvolcanic geothermal systems. It's the *scale*—the sheer volume of flowing water—that seems unbelievable. You need a powerful heat source to produce *this much* hot water. I'd expect to see something of this scale in the Yellowstone supervolcano or in Iceland's volcanic rift zone, but not in the middle of the Amazon, more than four hundred miles from the nearest active volcano. Where does all this water come from? Where does it get its heat? *How can this river exist?*

Geochemical water sampling at the Boiling River. This site, far upriver, is called the Mermaid's Waterfall. It is said to be home to a mermaid spirit.

I mark the location on my GPS. As expected, we're in the Agua Caliente Dome. I look south, worry crinkling my brow. About a mile and a half away is Peru's oldest Amazonian oil-field. *I sure hope this place is natural.* Just then, my aunt emerges from the cliff top near the Came Renaco. "I told you it was real!" she calls over the churning river.

Descending the stone steps, Guida makes her way to where I'm sitting, surrounded by my instruments. She relays that Maestro left for Pucallpa this morning with a big group of foreign patients and most of the Mayantuyacu community. She reassures me that we will meet him at the Pucallpa office tomorrow on our way back to the airport, but I worry. Now that I've seen the river, I need to understand it—and that means taking samples I can analyze back in the lab. Natural feature or not, the river is sacred to this community, and taking samples of their sacred waters without Maestro's permission is out of the question.

"So," she says, "what do you think?"

"It's amazing. I see it—but it's so incredible, I'm struggling to truly comprehend it." I pause. Then I blurt out, "I just *really* hope it's natural." I hadn't meant to voice my concern and immediately regret it.

Guida is surprised. "What do you mean?" she asks.

As a scientist, I tell her, when I'm confronted with something I don't understand, I try to come up with possible explanations—hypotheses. I can think of three that would account for the river. The waters could be heated by magma deep underground, like at Yellowstone— but this is unlikely here, as no study has ever identified any magma bodies in the area. The second explanation is that the waters are being heated by the earth itself. Even without local magma bodies, the earth's crust gets hotter the deeper down you go; we call this the geothermal gradient. If the waters are being heated by the geothermal gradient, then they are likely coming from deep in the earth. But waters cool as they flow up to the surface, so to have this much high-temperature water requires impressively fast flow rates from the bowels of the earth to the surface. Regardless of the cause, if it is natural, it is one of the largest geothermal features—volcanic or nonvolcanic—I've ever seen.

I hesitate, then explain the third hypothesis: that the river is not a natural phenomenon at all, that we're a mile and a half north of the oldest oilfield in the Peruvian Amazon. The river could be the result of an oilfield accident—an abandoned oil well producing hot water, or oilfield waters reinjected into the earth that are heating up and flowing out to the surface again. That's why I urgently need to find the 1933 Moran study, which might describe the river before human development began.

"Wow," Guida says softly. "So how do you find the answer?"

"First I need to ask Maestro's permission to study the river," I say. "It will take years to really understand this place, but step one is done—I know the river's exact location, and that its high temperatures aren't exaggerated." Guida casts me a smug smile.

"Once we're back in Lima, I'll review the studies of this area—fortunately, we're in a well-studied region. Then I'll try to contact the local oil company for information about their activities in this area.

"I want to come back for a longer stay next year, with a research team. I'm going to need help measuring the river's temperatures along its entire flow path to identify the river's pattern of heating."

"Pattern of heating?"

"Does it heat up at a single point or at multiple points over a larger area? If, *hypothetically*, the hot waters come from an old oil well, then there should be a single, major heating point where the old well is buried or hidden.

"For now, I'd like to take water samples. Waters have chemical 'fingerprints,' which can be analyzed in a lab to shed light on

Steep cliffs bound parts of the Boiling River. Together with thick jungle, this terrain can make field work a challenge. The environment demands that every step be intentional and well calculated; falling into the river below would have serious consequences.

things like whether they come from a known geothermal aquifer, or have magmatic or oilfield signatures. But I need permission first."

"What will you do if you find that it's an oilfield accident?" Guida asks uneasily.

"No idea—become very unpopular with the locals, I guess?" We laugh, but the idea turns my stomach. "Seriously, though," I say, "I'd do the right thing and report it."

"*Then* become very unpopular with the locals," Guida says. "And if it's natural?"

"Then I'll have proof that the world is more amazing than I could have ever imagined."

8 The Shaman

The half-moon wraps the jungle in its soft light, and the river roars its lullaby as a curtain of vapor rises from its waters. Hungry insects prowl outside my bed's mosquito net. Darkness conceals the world's distractions, leaving me alone with my thoughts.

I miss Sofía and struggle excitedly with how to tell her about today. I could fill volumes with the day's stories, experiences, and descriptions—but even then I'd have to summarize the journey's precious details. No story, no scientific study, no picture or video could ever do this place justice. Maybe that's why they say it's sacred.

Earlier today, Brunswick led us about a mile upriver, deep into the jungle. Every plant we passed had medicinal value, and each feature along the river was home to a different spirit. We saw large pools, one with a powerful waterfall about twenty feet tall—all with dangerously hot water.

Brunswick gave me permission to collect water samples, on the condition that I double-check with Maestro when we get to Pucallpa. He watched with interest as I carefully filled each bottle with scalding water and recorded every detail about each location.

Though I measured water temperatures up to 91°C (around 196°F), I discovered that the river begins as a cold stream. Along its path, it's supercharged at three major thermal injection zones. This heating pattern gives me hope that the river may be natural after all—if the water was flowing from an abandoned oil well, it would only be heated at a single point. But there is still the possibility of reinjected oilfield waters heating up and flowing to the surface through natural fault zones. I need more data before I can prove anything.

Far upstream, just before the first thermal injection zone, a great sandstone boulder resembling a serpent's head emerges from the jungle. Brunswick identified it as the most sacred site on the river, home to the Yacumama, or "Mother of the Waters"—a giant serpent spirit who births hot and cold waters. Beneath the great serpent rock's "jaws," a hot spring mixes with the cold stream water, bringing the legend to life.

Brunswick said the river has existed since before the time of the grandfathers, and that it represents both life and death. Death is everywhere here—early on our walk I saw an unfortunate frog fall into the river and boil alive. The river decorates itself with the bones of those who don't keep a respectful distance.

But in spite of the scalding waters, life abounds. Vegetation erupts from every patch of soil, and no matter where we looked something was crawling, calling, or slithering. I was taken aback to see algae growing in the river despite the near-boiling waters.

While I took water samples, Brunswick told me about the patients who come here to heal. Admittance is exclusively by word of mouth—the only way to be allowed in is if a "friend of Mayantuyacu" advocates for you, as Guida had done for me. Despite this, almost all the patients are foreign, chiefly Europeans

A victim of the river. The Boiling River here is around 80°C (176°F), and falling in at these temperatures means near-instant third-degree burns, muscles cooking on the bone, and no easy way out.

and North Americans. Brunswick also said that anthropologists and psychologists come to study Mayantuyacu's traditional healing methods and natural medicines. This must be the best-known unknown site in the world, I think, not for the first time.

But no one has ever come to study the river, Brunswick tells me. In the past people attributed the heat to the Yacumama spirit. Now, locals and foreigners just assume that the heat is from a volcano.

In the morning, the sun pierces the windows and holes in my wooden hut. I awaken to the harmonious sounds of the jungle. I meticulously pack my instruments and precious water samples for the long trip back to Lima.

Heading over to the kitchen hut, I see Brunswick and ask him where I can get some tea. He hands me a mug and a tea bag, then points down to the river. I laugh—but he indicates his own steaming mug. He is serious! Walking down to the river, I consider all the heavy metals and other nasty things, organic and inorganic, that are often found in geothermal waters. *Still, when in Rome...*

I dip my mug into the river and pull it out. Eddies of steam rise from the mug to caress my face as I peer in to see the clear, odorless water. Once it cools, I take my first sip. The water has a clean and pleasant taste. I drink my tea by the river, saying a private farewell before we retrace yesterday's journey and head back to the city.

Back in Pucallpa, Guida and I find ourselves standing before a familiar green door. I feel a surge of nervous excitement knowing Maestro Juan is just on the other side of this door. What will he have to say to me?

Guida knocks and soon the door swings open. A stout Amazonian woman stands before us.

"Sandra!" Guida exclaims. The old friends embrace, and Guida introduces me.

"We've heard a lot about you," Sandra says, taking me in. "It's not every day you meet someone interested in volcanoes and hot rivers. It's a bit odd. I'm just glad you didn't fall in!" Placing her hand on my arm, she says, "We know Guida would only bring us good people. Come in, please!" She leads us into the decorated office where our journey started yesterday.

A man gets up from his seat. He appears to be in his sixties.

He wears a Nike T-shirt, long brown shorts, long socks, and no shoes.

Though we are far from Mayantuyacu, I feel the jungle's presence in the room. His skin is the chocolate hue of the Pachitea, and his short hair and piercing eyes are as black as the forest night.

Maestro Juan gives me a reserved handshake. We take our seats. Guida and Sandra catch up while I sit in uncomfortable silence. Maestro remains as still as a stone, but he is clearly taking in every detail, and I can tell I'm being studied.

"Andrés, what did you think of Mayantuyacu?" Sandra asks me. I feel Maestro's serpentine gaze focus on me.

"Amazing," I manage. "The river is an absolute wonder—of Peru and of the world."

"A wonder?" Maestro breaks his silence, looking me in the eye. "And what makes a wonder?" he asks in a low, earthy voice, sitting forward in his seat.

"That's a good question," I say nervously. Then gesturing to the images on the walls, I say, "Look—the 'Wonders of Peru.' They are all special places. I've been lucky enough to see many of them, but Marcahuasi is the one I know best—I first went up when I was twelve."

His gaze narrows. "That is a far place to go for a twelve-year-old."

"It's important to my family," I reply.

"Dr. Daniel Ruzo."

"Yes! How did you know?"

"I once went up to Marcahuasi for a few days to study—to

learn from the dead," he says solemnly. "Dr. Daniel Ruzo is very respected by the people of Marcahuasi."

"He was my great-grandfather," I say. "He died when I was very young, so I never really got to know him. But he loved Marcahuasi, and I feel connected to him there."

Maestro's gaze softens. "It is important to connect with the ancestors."

I nod in agreement. "I felt very connected to him recently when his widow gave me some of his old things." I pause, smiling at the memory. "Something funny happened that day. When she learned I had become a geologist, she laughed and said, 'There is no single group of people whom your great-grandfather detested more than geologists!' Then she looked up to heaven and said, 'See, Daniel? Karma!'"

"Why karma?" Maestro asks.

"Well, my great-grandfather had his own ideas about what carved the monoliths of Marcahuasi. Geologists disagreed with him, and it didn't bring out the best in him—to put it nicely."

A toothy grin spreads across Maestro's face. "So who do you honor—your great-grandfather, or his *friends*?"

"I don't think it's about honoring either group," I reply. "It's about honoring Marcahuasi. Nature tells its own story. Sometimes we misread it—but there is a difference between being open to any outcome and only looking for the one you want. I say this respectfully, but my great-grandfather was not a scientist, and in his writings he seems more interested in proving his point than listening to nature."

Maestro smiles. "The plants teach us to heal people. We

must listen to them to make the medicines. You can hurt people if you don't listen properly." He pauses again. "Why do you study geology?"

"Well, I love being outside," I say with a smile. "But really, I feel that geology gives me the best chance to save the world, as I use it to try to find better ways to produce energy and resources.

"I'm blessed to call three countries my own: Peru, Nicaragua, and the United States. They're very different places, but they have similar needs, such as clean air and water, economic stability, a healthy society—all of which are tied, either directly or indirectly, to how we use our natural resources. So if we find better ways to produce and use our energy and resources we simultaneously work to solve these other issues. In the end, I think that if we take care of nature, she will take care of us. And geology is my way of honoring her."

For a long time—uncomfortably long—Maestro does not respond. Finally a smile snakes across his face and he bursts into a laugh.

"I understand now," he says tenderly. "I am a *curandero* (healer) of humanity—my mission is to heal people. You are a *curandero* of the earth—your mission is to heal it. Nature belongs to all countries, and is not confined by borders—and neither are you, my young doctor. You were made for this mission, and so were born a twin soul to nature herself. It is important for you to do your studies, and you have my blessing to study at Mayantuyacu."

I am speechless.

"Good surprise, no?" Maestro laughs again.

I thank him profusely and express my hope to return soon. "Maestro, one more thing—" I say.

"Yes?"

I pull out a plastic grocery bag containing the water samples. "I collected these samples yesterday. I wanted to ask your permission first, but because you weren't there I consulted with Brunswick, who said to bring them to you and ask if I could take them."

"You already have your permission," he says softly, pulling out a bottle and contemplating it. "Thank you for showing me these. You're a good kid." Then, standing up, he says, "I have something for you." He disappears into an adjacent room and reemerges with something in his hand. He drops it into mine. It's cold with smooth undulations. "It's an *encanto* from the jungle—a talisman for protection on your mission."

A fossilized oyster. It fits perfectly in the palm of my hand. "Thank you," I say, admiring the smooth texture of the gray shell.

"There is one more thing I want to ask of you," Maestro says. Again he picks up one of the water samples. "After you study the waters, pour them out onto the ground, wherever you are in the world, so the waters can find their way back home."

9 A Long-Awaited Return

Night falls on Mayantuyacu, and the jungle teems with life. Bats emerge from their roosts, maneuvering through the darkness with their otherworldly pitches. Frogs and insects belt out their songs. Spiders' eyes shine like dew as they move through the jungle. Looming over it all, vividly present even in the dark, is the river—bellowing out its roar, filling the cool night air with billowing clouds.

The revving of an electric generator interrupts the nighttime chorus and overwhelms the organic noises. The lightbulbs flicker on in the maloca—the large, traditional Amazonian long-house at the center of the Mayantuyacu community.

It's July 2012, and I'm back in the jungle after eight months in Dallas. Organizing this fieldwork season was an uphill battle. My doctoral committee was concerned that the Boiling River was becoming a distraction. "You're so far along in your geothermal mapping work"—one committee member told me—"putting it on hold to study this river, which will likely take years of study to do it right, seems like a bad idea."

Fortunately my committee chair was not afraid to let me make my own mistakes—something I will forever be grateful for—and I obtained the permissions I needed. But at that point, the time was too short to secure the funding I had hoped for. I broke the piggy bank to personally buy the tools

I needed, and cashed in frequent flyer miles to get back to the river.

After a long day traveling into the jungle, our eclectic eight-person volunteer research team sits in a circle on the maloca's wooden floor. Among us we count two geoscientists, a filmmaker, an architecture student, a video game artist, a raptor handler, an advertiser, and a primary school teacher. No one but me has been to the Amazon before, and the group buzzes with excitement as the others compare their reactions.

"This place is more beautiful than I ever imagined!" exclaims my wife, Sofía, who just completed her master's in advertising at SMU.

My cousin Poncho, the video game artist, agrees. "The pictures were amazing, but seeing it in real life—*wow!*"

"It feels like a movie set," says Carlos, who works at a raptor rehabilitation center.

"What is most impressive is the size of the river," says Maria, the only other geoscientist in the group. "I've seen hot springs all over, but something this big—it's hard to comprehend how much hot water there is."

"I still can't believe the shaman now has a website," says Peter, the filmmaker. "Next thing you know he'll be on Facebook!"

"And the one thing they asked us to bring from Lima was a box of donuts," says Basil, an architecture student and Peter's younger brother.

Whitney, the primary school teacher, says, "Thank you for letting us be a part of this!"

As we sit chatting idly, I suddenly realize that the generator only runs for two hours a night. Calling the group's attention, I delve into what our work here will entail.

"For the next month we'll be in the jungle, trying to understand how this boiling—or near-boiling—river can exist more than four hundred miles from the nearest active volcanic center. There are three main hypotheses.

"The first is that the river is related to a magmatic system. At this point, I think we can rule this hypothesis out: this area has been well studied, geologically, with no record of anything volcanic or magmatic. Furthermore, analysis of the 2011 water samples indicates that the river's waters are meteoric—they have the same chemical fingerprint as waters that fall to earth as rain or snow. But I took those samples during peak wet season, which might have influenced the results. That's why we're here during peak dry season—to sample the "purest" geothermal waters we can get.

The second hypothesis—what makes this discovery so exciting—is that the river is the result of an abnormally large hydrothermal system, where water seeps deep into the earth and heats up before springing to the surface. It's a phenomenon that occurs regularly, but given these temperatures and the tremendous amount of hot water, well, the rates must be incredibly high. We could very well be looking at the largest, or at least one of the largest, nonvolcanic continental geothermal surface features in the world. This is exciting in itself, but understanding this system could yield an even more important result."

The team looks at me, expressions confused, except for Maria, who smiles, nodding. She knows where I'm going with this.

The 2012 Boiling River Expedition Team: Andrés, Sofía, Peter, Whitney, Maria, Basil, Carlos, and Poncho. The large pool behind us is about 60°C (140°F).

"This place is sacred and should never be developed," I begin slowly, "but it's worth considering that the same processes that create the Boiling River might also be creating other geothermal systems, buried deep underground in other parts of the Amazon. If these systems can be harnessed for geothermal energy, they could help growing Amazonian cities like Pucallpa lower their environmental footprint, as well as provide jobs."

"Again, this river should never be harnessed," I repeat, "but understanding how it works could ideally help us find harmony between the current modern standards of living and the natural world."

Finally, the third hypothesis. I lower my voice: "Worst-case scenario is that the river might not be natural. It could be the result of an oilfield accident."

"What about the legends?" Whitney asks.

"The legends could have come later," I say. "It's not uncommon for unusual features to have significance retroactively attributed to them. The Boiling River is not identified in any studies I can find. The area has been explored and developed for about eighty years. So there's an elephant in the room: *why wasn't it identified before?*

"There is one study that could hold the key to this question, but I can't find it anywhere—the 1933 Moran study. It's the only study done prior to any development here, and in theory it should identify the river. I've also been trying to reach Maple Gas, the oil company that's operating in this area, but no luck on that front either. My hope is they'll let me explore their oilfield— for my geothermal mapping, and to better understand this river.

"Regardless, our goal for this trip is to study the river in detail. The main objectives are to take the water samples and to make a detailed temperature map of the river as it flows to the Pachitea. Unfortunately, the Google Earth satellite imagery for this area is so low-resolution that it's of no use. I'm petitioning Google headquarters for support to get high-res imagery.

"Before we end this meeting, I want to add that Maestro Juan and Sandra are in Pucallpa and will be back in three days with a big group of tourists. That should be everything. Any questions, comments, or concerns?"

"Just one," Carlos says. "I just realized this is the farthest I have ever been from a slice of pizza."

Sofía and I prepare for bed in our hut at the edge of the community as the generator is cut and darkness returns to the jungle. I meticulously tuck the edges of our mosquito net under our mattress.

"I still can't believe how much they have bitten you," Sofía says. "It's so weird. We're all using the same insect repellent . . ."

As we settle into bed, I say, "*Amor*, I don't get it."

"Get what?"

"Brunswick was telling me that virtually no Peruvians come here—the tourists are almost all foreign. I looked through the guest book, and it's true, they're from all over the world. I'm just dumbfounded that no one has ever investigated why there's a massive thermal river in the middle of the Amazon."

"Andrés," she says softly. "You are a geothermal scientist— these things naturally stand out to you. These tourists come here to heal; they're focused on their own issues and emotions.

And sudden immersion in the middle of the Amazon is pretty overwhelming, especially if you're coming from a developed country. It's a lot to take in. Everyone sees the river as special and unusual, but *everything* about this place seems special and unusual. And these days it feels like every corner of the globe has been explored. It's very easy to assume that someone has already investigated it, especially if you're not an expert."

"You're right," I reply. "I forget that not everyone shares my perspective. In science we are pushed to scrutinize, to seek significance in what we don't understand. I just wish people would challenge their assumptions more—it would help them realize what an amazing world we live in."

"That's why we have scientists like you," Sofía replies. "Now, please—I'm exhausted."

I stare into the darkness, my mind swirling with all that lies ahead of us tomorrow, and all that we might discover. Unable to keep my thoughts in, I say, "I just feel so honored that Maestro is letting me study the river and bring it to the world." But Sofía has drifted off to sleep.

10 The Ceremony

The first three days of fieldwork go smoothly: reconnaissance work along the river, calibrating instruments, and field testing methodologies to ensure the greatest possible accuracy. As promised, Maestro and Sandra return with the new guests. I catch up with Maestro, who is preparing plant medicines near the river.

"We made it upriver, where the river is just a cold stream, to a cold pool with a waterfall that you can sit behind," I report. "But we couldn't get past this waterfall—the jungle was too thick."

"Luis will take you," Maestro says. "He knows the jungle best."

"That would be great," I reply. "The terrain and dense vegetation are even causing problems for our GPS units. The location error is too high to be useful, unless we're in a clearing, which isn't very common."

"What will you do?" Maestro asks without lifting his eyes from his work.

"I am going to tie Poncho and Carlos together with a eleven-yard rope," I tell him. "Starting as far upriver as we can, we'll measure the river's temperatures every eleven yards until we've walked its entire length."

Maestro finds this hysterical. Once he has stopped laughing, he inspects my bug bites. "They have bitten you a lot."

I look at my arms and legs. "They are eating me alive! I

counted seventy-six bites on just one leg, then stopped counting. What's weird is that our entire group is using the same repellent, but no one else looks like this."

"I imagined this would happen," Maestro says. "The jungle is trying to protect herself."

"From what?"

"From you."

"What about everyone else in my group?" I ask.

"They don't pose a threat," he says. "The jungle is afraid of you. The spirits of the jungle see inside of us. From the time you arrived, the jungle has been watching you. It sees into your mind, sees the knowledge you possess. People with your knowledge have come into this jungle before, and the jungle was hurt by it."

The elusive Moran study flashes in my mind. Though I haven't read it, I know it brought the first oil development to the Peruvian Amazon.

"But what about Maria?"

"She has no roots here and is not a threat."

I take a breath, then ask, "What can I do to make it right?"

"The jungle needs to see your soul," Maestro says evenly. Then, looking at the river, he continues. "The river called you here for a purpose—a purpose it will show in time. Before, I did not understand the river's purpose for you. Now it is the jungle who doesn't understand. We fear what we don't understand. So tonight we introduce you to the jungle."

That night, I make my way to the maloca, at the center of the community, where Maestro told me the ceremony would take place. I'm a little anxious as I enter. But as I step inside, a familiar smell instantly puts me at ease. The maloca is filled with the sweet-smelling smoke of *palo santo* wood. The scent evokes childhood memories of my dad using *palo santo* in our home for prayer. A calm washes through me, and I step forward.

Brunswick holds the incense bowl, whose fires light the darkness. The firelight reveals Maestro and Brunswick in traditional ceremonial *kushmas*, the long Asháninka ponchos with blue, red, and green vertical stripes, and top-brimmed headdresses with long scarlet macaw tail feathers. In one hand Maestro holds a long-necked green bottle; in the other, a lit *mapacho* cigarette of strong, wild Amazonian tobacco.

The glow of the bowl's fire and the *mapacho*'s burning red cherry are intensified by the darkness, illuminating the faces of the shaman and his apprentice as they prepare the room for the ceremony. I kneel, keeping my back straight, as Brunswick approaches with the incense bowl. He blows out the fire, leaving only a billowing mass of glowing red embers, and holds the bowl about a foot in front of me as Maestro begins to chant.

Icaros! The spells of the Amazonians! Guida and Eo told me about *icaros* back in Lima. They can heal or guide, invoke or conjure, summon or conceal, transform or shape, attack or defend. Here in the darkness, I hear them chanted by a master.

With his free hand, Brunswick signals for me to spread the fragrant incense over myself. With cupped hands, I trap the smoke as it billows out of the bowl and do as instructed. Spreading the thick, sweet smoke over and around my body, I feel a gentle warmth hugging my exposed skin, which proves unexpectedly satisfying. In the red glow, I watch the smoke

Maestro Juan comes from a long line of Asháninka *curanderos* (healers). Aided by medicinal plants and the thermal waters of the Boiling River, he uses the knowledge of his grandfathers to pursue his mission of healing humanity.

catch momentarily in the folds of my shirt and pants before dissipating.

Maestro sings a rhythmic and haunting *icaro* in an unfamiliar Amazonian tongue, sometimes using words, sometimes only melodies. The chant feels as old as the jungle itself. As he continues to sing, the song changes subtly. The sounds Maestro makes closely resemble the familiar sounds of the jungle.

After a few minutes, the *icaro* begins to fade, ending with a sharp whistled exhale. The maloca is silent save for the river, which roars out its own *icaro* in the darkness. Sparks from a lighter flash as Maestro relights his *mapacho*.

Now Brunswick begins his own *icaro*, a religious hymn about Jesus appearing in the clouds. The words are Spanish, but the rhythm is unmistakably Amazonian—a fascinating blend of Catholicism and Amazonian spirituality.

Maestro stoops in front of me, holding out his left hand. He signals toward my hands and I hold them out in a prayer position. Cupping my hands together, he takes a drag of the *mapacho* and blows the musky smoke into my hands in whistled exhales. He repeats this on my hands, then again on the crown of my head.

Brunswick's *icaro* begins to fade. After another brief pause, Maestro begins another *icaro*. He sings in Spanish, mixed with an indigenous tongue that's not the one he used in his first *icaro*. Listening intently, I can distinguish certain words, which have clear Quechua roots—but not the Andean Quechua I am used to. Maestro invokes the spirits of the water and the vapor, the jungle and its plants, and finally God and the angels. When he sings to the waters his tone is warm and familiar, as if he is speaking to a beloved family member. When he sings to God, I feel a deep reverence. But when he sings to the jungle and the plants it is as if he is trying to convince them of something. I can tell he is advocating on my behalf.

He names the important trees, the Came Renaco first among them, and he praises each for its powerful medicine. After each tree's name he sings a distinct tune, specific to that tree. I imagine he is showing each of the guardian trees that he knows them. Maestro closes each tree's *icaro* with the words *llora, llora, como yo* (cries, cries, just like me), as if to remind each tree that he recognizes its life and respects its spirit as the equal of his own.

Maestro finishes with another series of whistled exhales. He then lifts the thin green bottle and sprinkles me with its contents—a flowery perfume with a pleasant and delicate scent. He signals to me to hold out my hands in a prayer position as before. He places his mouth over the bottle's opening and takes in a deep breath of the flowery perfume, then, in the same whistled exhales he expels his flowery breath into my hands, onto both of my shoulders, and onto the crown of my head.

Maestro steps back. By the light of the embers I see a smile flicker across his face. He nods slowly and I rise.

"Find me tomorrow morning," he says in a low voice. "There is a place I need to show you."

11 Spirits of the Jungle

"Things will be different for you now," Maestro says solemnly. We walk upriver in the early morning sun. "The river baptized you with vapor. Yesterday, we baptized you with plants. The jungle now knows you are not a threat—that you are here to help."

I give him an incredulous look, but he just smiles. "Have you been bitten?" he asks.

I inspect my arms and legs. There are no new bites. I pause, trying to remember. Had I reapplied my repellent? No, I bathed before the ceremony and didn't apply new repellent afterward. Maestro smiles knowingly.

"They won't bother you anymore," Maestro says.

"How do you know?"

He pauses, his dark eyes twinkling, and says, "You have your science, I have mine."

As we walk, I puzzle over Maestro's words: *baptized with vapor and now baptized with plants.*

Then it dawns on me: *palo santo* is a wood, tobacco is a leaf, and the perfume is made of flowers. Each represents a different part of a plant. The river's vapor had been mirrored last night by the burning plant's smoke.

Maestro and Brunswick stop walking and turn to the edge of the path. With their machetes they begin to clear an old, overgrown trail down a steep slope. We can hear the river surging below us, but it's concealed by dense vegetation. I follow their lead, and we work our way down the slope to a stone riverbank.

Here the river is around twenty-five feet wide. The turquoise waters are beautifully clear, and the current is steady and strong. The sun beats down on us and the riverbank feels hotter than normal, leaving Maestro, Brunswick, and me dripping with sweat.

The river sounds different here—its roar replaced by the trickle of a myriad of streams. Many of the riverbank's ivory-colored stones are stained by rust-colored paths upon which flow steaming streams of clear water, flanked on either side by bands of green and yellow (likely algae or bacterial mats). Where the geothermal waters spring from the ground, mineral deposits have formed fantastic shapes reminiscent of marine corals. It's a geothermal scientist's paradise.

Maestro notices my excitement. "These are the Sacred Waters. Powerful spirits live here," he says solemnly. "They are pure and very hot. Use your feet like eyes to know where to step. Look around, but be very careful."

I investigate the springs as Maestro and Brunswick begin cutting another trail at the river's edge.

About fifteen minutes pass before Maestro calls me. He and Brunswick's figures appear as silhouettes through the heavy steam. They are about twenty yards downstream, standing in single file on their newly cleared trail.

The thin trail is on the knife-edge where the steep slope falls abruptly into the river below. One foot in front of the other,

I very carefully make my way to them. Where the trail is not muddy it is covered by freshly cut vegetation, which proves to be slippery. Occasional breezes surround me with steam, limiting my vision.

I focus on walking. Sweat pours down my face. Each breath is slow and deep, each step calculated and firm.

Finally I reach Maestro and Brunswick. Only then do I notice the churning, splashing sound. Through the thick, humid air and suffocating heat, I see a large patch of water less than a foot below us, churning violently.

"This is La Bomba," Maestro says. (The Pump.) "Be extremely careful here."

His warning is unnecessary. The heat is intense—almost unbearable—and it feels significantly hotter than any other spot I've been to on the river. In spite of the sweltering day, thick clouds of vapor rise from the river, forcing us to squint to protect our eyes from the searing hot air. I have never seen so much thermal water with such a powerful flow rate—and certainly not from such a precarious position. One slip would mean instant third-degree burns, and I'd have no easy way out of the current. Bubbles erupt across the water's surface and a plume of vapor rises thickly above. There is no room for a misstep, nor the distraction of a needless thought. Instinct fills me with a clear-headedness dominated by a singular focus: every breath, every step, every thought is intentional and calculated. There is no room for error.

I know I don't have much time here, but I urgently want to understand this bizarre system. One by one, I begin adding up the facts before me: the density of the white vapor in spite of hot air temperatures, the intensity of the bursting bubbles, the almost unbearable heat. Through squinted eyes, I scan the scene beyond the violently bubbling patch of water. I notice that the river's surface breaks in many places as if raindrops were falling on it—but there is no rain, only bubbles from below. My eyes follow faults, linear cracks in rock, down the cliff on the opposite side of the river and into the water below. The bubbles were coming from the faults! Faults often serve as earth's "arteries," superhighways for water flowing through the earth. This is exactly what is happening here—the river is being heated by fault-fed hot springs.

I am in awe. Wasn't this supposed to be a legend? An exaggeration?

In disbelief, I turn to the bubbling water. I can't be certain if the odorless, colorless gas is just water vapor or something more exotic. I'm devising how I can get a sample, and wishing I had brought my thermometer. I need hard data to confirm what I'm seeing. Is the river really boiling?

A voice plays in my head: *Andrés, if you were a scared conquistador lost in the jungle, you wouldn't be running around with a thermometer. And you know exactly what you would call this.* The uncertainty fades, and I let myself savor the moment, relishing every breath of painfully hot air.

For a long time, I had secretly hoped the Boiling River would live up to its name, and in this moment of discovery it has—qualitatively at least. I still need to quantitatively confirm the temperature measurements, but for now I stand mesmerized by

La Bomba's churning, bubbling waters, thrilled and relieved in equal measure.

I could stay looking at the river for hours, but Maestro and Brunswick politely express their eagerness to escape the suffocating heat. Single file, we slowly, carefully retrace the knife-edge trail back to the Sacred Waters. Back on the secure stone bank, I profusely thank Maestro for bringing me here. "But there is one thing I don't understand," I press. "If this part of the river is so special, why were the paths so overgrown?"

Maestro smiles like a teacher whose student has asked the right question. "We conceal to protect," he explains. "This river is sacred. In churches, the smoke from incense and candles takes the faithful's prayers up to God—here, it is the river's vapor that carries the prayers of the animals, plants, rocks, and all creation. It is a natural church.

"Long ago, in the time of the grandfathers, almost no one came here. People were afraid of the river's spirits and only the most powerful *curanderos* would come.

"The grandfathers had a deep respect for this river. But times change. The Great Civilization has brought its progress to the jungle, and now only a few old people even remember its legitimate name: Shanay-timpishka." (Boiled by the heat of the sun.) "It is tempting to fall under the spell of the modern. It almost called to me, but the river called me with more force."

"What happened?" I ask.

"Walking through the jungle, I fell into a hunter's trap and was shot. The hospital doctors said I would never walk again. I still have the scars." He points to his legs and feet, and I understand why Maestro always wears socks or long pants that cover his lower legs.

"But you walk perfectly," I marvel. "How did you heal?"

"Sandra," he says with a smile. "She was my nurse at the hospital, and she told me, 'If you are such a great shaman, why don't you heal yourself?' She called me to be better than myself. She was right.

"With some help from friends and crutches, I left the hospital and came to this place, remembering the stories the grandfathers once told of the spirits of the jungle and the powerful medicines. The Came Renaco gave me its medicine, and together with the vapor of the river, my bones and muscles began to heal. They said I would never walk again—but I proved that the ancient medicines still have their value. The Great Civilization too often underestimates the power of the plant, and even our youth forget. This is why we founded Mayantuyacu—so that the ancient study of the plants is not lost."

That evening I sit alone under the Came Renaco, watching the river surge past.

"Boiled by the heat of the sun," I whisper aloud, thinking of the Amazonians who long ago gave the river this name. I'm not the first to wonder why the river boils.

To the ancient Amazonians, the river being sun-boiled was the best hypothesis. Now their descendants think it is volcanic. So far, my data suggest a powerful hydrothermal system. Maybe one day, my "advanced" scientific understanding of the river will seem as limited an explanation as the sun boiling it into existence.

A dark thought crosses my mind: *I still haven't ruled out the oilfield accident hypothesis.* Oral traditions are not considered accurate scientific documentation. I *need* to find the Moran study—with luck the river is documented, and I'll finally know if it existed before development.

The thought is gut-wrenching. This place and its people have become important to me. I feel that it is a special place—but will the data tell the same story?

Running my hand across my bare arms and legs, I notice no new bug bites. Maybe I just can't tell the new bites from the old—or perhaps some chemical in Maestro's perfume works as a natural repellent. There must be a scientific explanation. But I can't escape the fact that something is different: the ceremony seems to have worked.

I look back to the river, trying to understand this limbo in which I find myself—a place where science and spirituality appear to coexist in harmony.

The rest of the month passes quickly. On the eve of our departure, I seek out Maestro to say good-bye and find him in his hammock, smoking a *mapacho*. I pull up a plastic stool next to him and open my computer to show him the graph of the river's temperatures along its flow path.

"Here are the temperatures we measured," I explain. "We made it as far upriver as we could, but Luis did not want to go all the way to the source. He said there are spirits that appear to you in the form of a family member before taking you away."

"*Shapishicus*," Maestro says. "They can be nasty. Better that you didn't go." I smile, wondering how my doctoral committee will take this explanation.

"As you can see in the graph," I continue, "the river starts off cold, then heats up, cools, heats up again, cools a little, then heats up to its maximum temperature, before slowly cooling along its path before crashing into the Pachitea. Unfortunately we couldn't measure the entire river—the jungle was too thick. But I'll come back for that. For now, these data show multiple injection zones, where hot water pours out of fault zones, boosting the river's temperature and volume. My hope is that by comparing these data with the rock and water analyses, I'll be able to chemically identify individual aquifers the fault zones tap into. There is much more work to do."

Maestro studies the graph and points to the temperature peaks. "I have never seen the Yacumama, Sumiruna's Pool, and the Sacred Waters like this before," he says. I realize that the sites that are scientifically significant for me independently hold deep spiritual meaning for Maestro.

He smiles approvingly. "This is good and important work. Thank you." I'm euphoric.

"One more thing," I say, reaching into my backpack. "I found this in the jungle with Luis." I show him a pair of oyster fossils that have been naturally cemented together into a heart shape.

"An *encanto,*" Maestro says. "I've never seen one like this." He contemplates it, then says softly, "The jungle has given you her heart. Take good care of it."

The bubbling Sacred Waters. Faults—fractures in the earth—serve as "arteries" that allow geothermal waters to flow to the surface and create the Boiling River.

12 The Smoking Gun

"Disturbing on first observation . . ."

R. G. Greene, a colleague of Robert B. Moran and Douglas Fyfe,
on encountering the Boiling River in the early 1930s.
Moran Papers. 1936.

It's February 2013, and I'm at the SMU Geothermal Lab in Texas, analyzing the Boiling River samples in a cold, windowless lab. In the six months since I last left the Amazon, I've found my mind regularly drifting back to the river and its jungle. Maestro said that the jungle had "given me her heart"—and it's clear to me that I had left her a piece of mine.

The Boiling River is not a legend—but it does seem out of a dream. Its hot waters flow for about four miles, getting more than six feet deep in places, and up to eighty feet wide in others. The river boasts large thermal pools, scalding rapids, steaming waterfalls, and boiling hot springs—and all this, in a non-volcanic geothermal system, over four hundred miles from the nearest active volcanic center.

But a threat still looms like a nightmare—could the sacred river be an oilfield accident? After all, how could such a large geothermal feature go undocumented and "unnoticed" in such a well-studied, well-visited area? Why had this large, culturally significant, thermal river never been properly identified? Though Maestro and other older members of the community insist that the river has existed "since before the time of the grandfathers," there is no definitive proof. Finding the Moran and Fyfe report is more important than ever now. It's the only document that can answer whether or not the Boiling River existed prior to oilfield development.

I walk over to my lab computer and type "Moran and Fyfe" into the search engine for what seems like the millionth time. Over the years, I had unsuccessfully sent various combinations of related keywords into the virtual void. I pause, waiting for the queries to load. Unbelievably, this time there is a hit. I lean in close and read the title: "Guide to the Robert B. and William R. Moran Papers."

In the flurry of a few clicks, I'm taken into the Online Archive of California, where I discover the archival breakdown of a collection of original reports, writings, photographs, and other documents belonging to Robert B. Moran—collectively referred to as the "Moran Papers."

After two years of searching, here it is: a lead on the *actual* Moran report. Neither the report nor any documents from the Moran Papers are visible online. But the website indicates that the Moran Papers are kept in the closed archives of the University of California, Santa Barbara (UCSB) Special Collections Library. Then I hit a dead end: the archives can only be accessed with special legal permission from the Moran Trust.

I call the library. A quiet "hello" from the librarian on the other end of the line triggers a passionate account of my search for the Moran Papers and the huge relief that the search might finally be over. I pause to breathe. There is an awkward silence. I quickly realize the librarian was ill-prepared for the tenor of this conversation when he picked up the phone. Suddenly embarrassed, I will my voice to calm.

"Good afternoon. My name is Andrés Ruzo, I am a doctoral student from Southern Methodist University, and I am calling regarding obtaining access to the Moran Trust Archives for purposes relating to my geophysical research in Peru."

There is a pause, then, "For the Moran Papers, you will need to contact the trust's lawyer."

Ten long days pass before I hear from the lawyer, but at last I get my answer. Soon, I'm on a plane to Santa Barbara.

"This is the viewing room." A kind, soft-spoken librarian leads me to a large, rectangular room in the UCSB Special Collections Library. "No food or drink is allowed here, and the documents *cannot* leave this room. Find a table and I'll bring the cart with the Moran Papers archival boxes to you." She leaves me alone in the room, but not before adding, "Oh, and please remember—this is a *quiet* room."

As a geoscientist, "archival work" brings to mind poorly lit, windowless rooms, generally in buildings that could easily pass for abandoned warehouses, full of long, heavy trays filled with rock samples. Rock libraries are rarely the cleanest places; you often leave covered in dust and badly in need of a shower. By contrast, my archival work here feels luxurious. The viewing room is immaculately neat. The long fluorescent lights overhead illuminate subdued neutral colors that seem to enhance the silence and stillness. Ten tables, each with a single chair, fill the room—a reminder that work is to be done alone, and quietly.

A series of identical, ancient card catalogs, six feet tall, stretch across the entire length of the back wall. Hundreds of regularly spaced drawer knobs and labels reinforce the room's sense of order. Atop the card catalog, taciturn busts watch over the room. Nearby, a ceramic, life-size Jack Russell terrier stares into an old gramophone. But the room's most distinctive features are the large windows that cover the remaining walls. They inspire the feeling of being in a fishbowl, where the archive-viewer is viewed, in turn, by watchful librarians from almost every angle.

I choose my table just as the librarian returns with a multi-level metal cart. The old cart bears a number of gray archival boxes, each with a red ribbon securing its lid. I'm told I can only enter the room with one box at a time. I gingerly lift the first of the numbered boxes in the series, keenly aware of the librarian's scrutinizing gaze as I walk into the viewing room. I comb through the box with great care, meticulously checking every document, before rewrapping it with its red ribbon, and carrying it back out of the room to exchange it for another. This goes on for hours. Most of the contents are personal items: postcards, opera playbills, or other nongeologic information.

As I lift the lid off Box 89, a label instantly catches my attention: "Agua Caliente, Peru, Geologic Reports." My breath catches. It's like seeing a ghost. Gently, I lift the folder out of the box and open slowly to unveil a stack of old, yellowed papers. Here and there, the typewritten text is annotated in a handwritten cursive of a time gone by. As I look through the creased pages a wave of uncontrollable joy washes over me—I found it. I'm holding not only the 1933 study I've sought for so long, but a whole trove of unpublished notes and reports that puts the study in its historical context—invaluable insight into the earliest stages of exploration and development on the Agua Caliente Dome. The answer to whether or not the river existed *before* oilfield development is hidden in these pages.

It's midmorning, and through my fishbowl, I see UCSB students walking the halls and diligently working in the library. *Amazing*, I think to myself. I've spent years looking for this information, and flown halfway across the country just to be in this library. But to these students this library is just as much a part of their everyday as SMU is to me, or the river is to Mayantuyacu. Then a thought takes hold: what discoveries lie hidden in the white noise of my own life, lost in my own everyday landscape? The fishbowl's large wall clock chides me back to the pages in my hand. The Moran Papers tell a fascinating story of the unrestrained early days of Amazonian oil exploration.

In the 1920s and 1930s, the Peruvian Amazon was in the crosshairs of international oil development. Standard Oil of New Jersey and the Rockefeller Foundation were sending teams of geologists into the jungle, and secrecy was paramount.

It was during this time that geologist Robert B. Moran, came across a large, oval-shaped landform while doing an aerial survey for a railroad construction project—a geologic dome, rising hundreds of feet above the flat, low jungle.

Moran quickly identified the dome as an ideal place to find

oil and swiftly organized a team to investigate the area between 1930 and 1932.

Though there are no original field notes in the archives, I find numerous field reports, compiled long after their team's time in the Amazon was over. The reports tell a perplexing story. Moran and his team *had* found the river. However, inconsistencies within their reports confuse me—some match my own observations of the river, but others do not. In those that don't, it seems as if the river is being purposely underplayed. I'm well aware that their focus was finding oil, not studying the Boiling River— but still, something doesn't seem right. Fortunately an internal report by geologist R. G. Greene presents a compelling explanation for the inconsistencies. Greene was a third-party contractor called in to check the work of Moran and his team. This is still a common practice in the oil industry—getting a third-party expert to confirm a company's geologic work, often for the sake of potential investors (who regularly have no technical geologic knowledge whatsoever).

Greene states, "The presence of hot water is rather disturbing on first observation, but after analysis lends itself to a satisfactory interpretation other than that of an hot intrusive magma, *the presence of which, naturally would be detrimental to the prospective value of the Agua Caliente anticline.*"

This was the smoking gun. Maestro was right—the river *had* existed since before the time of the grandfathers. Moran's team *had* found the river, and their observations generally matched mine—supporting the hypothesis that the site has not been significantly impacted by oilfield development. They found the river at a time long before modern regulations would have demanded that the interests of the environment or "wild Indians" (as one report called them) be taken into account or even reported. The jungle still hides the river well, so it is easy to imagine how a "reporting oversight" could pass from one operating oil company to another over the decades, even after modern regulations were put in place. Lastly, the team's focus was producing oil and obtaining investors.

Geothermal systems are often seen as a threat to oil resources as they can "overcook" them, leaving them ruined and worthless. Moran and his team's proprietary 1930s geologic work confirms that the river is *not* magmatic, and that it poses no threat to the oil resources. However, trying to explain all this to non-expert, easily spooked investors, holding the purse strings to essential funding, seems like a daunting task. It's no longer a surprise that the river receives so little attention in the Moran Papers, and though properly described in some reports, it seems underplayed in others.

Fortunately for Moran and his colleagues, their efforts paid off. They formalized an oil concession with the Peruvian government, and by 1938 had successfully drilled the first oil well in the Peruvian Amazon.

Here, at last, is my evidence. The river *is* a natural phenomenon that existed *before* oilfield development. I sit down hard in my chair, mind bursting with all that must be done and the questions that remain unanswered.

13 The Greatest Threat

It is August 2013, almost a year to the day since I last left the jungle. I am in a truck labeled MAPLE GAS COMPANY, ready to spend a week working on the Agua Caliente Dome.

Maple Gas is allowing me to conduct my research on their oilfield. They have given me full access to any data, maps, and samples I need, as well as permission to take deep-earth temperature measurements in their wells. This information gives me a far better understanding of the geology and tectonic forces in the area, and access to Maple's wells means I can get an unprecedented look at the deep-earth temperatures around the Boiling River. Maple also gives me essential operations data, which further illustrates that the river is a natural feature, unimpacted by oilfield activities. Furthermore, to my doctoral committee's delight, the data from those wells will make it possible to determine the first high-quality heat flow sites in the Peruvian Amazon—bringing me one step closer to creating the first detailed geothermal map of Peru.

As we drive, I look out the window. Rolling hills, grassy pastures, and the occasional ruminating cows as far as the eye can see.

"Sad, isn't it?" says José, Maple's geologist. I look at him, confused.

"Watch the landscape between here and the oilfield—there is

an environmental catastrophe happening in plain sight and no one seems to give a damn," José continues. "This is the Amazon rain forest. There shouldn't be vast grassy plains."

I look out on the pastures again. José is right. I've passed these lands every year since I first came to the river—how had I missed this detail? When I thought of deforestation I'd always imagined a barren wasteland of mud, tractor trails, and tree stumps—not picturesque rolling pastureland. I can't believe I hadn't seen what was right in front of me. An angry queasiness blooms in my gut.

José is in his early forties and has worked in oilfields all over Peru. He has a laid-back, jovial demeanor that belies a no-nonsense authority. "The frustrating thing is that people still love to hate

Post-apocalyptic Amazonia: rolling plains, ruminating cows, and the charred remains of a once virgin jungle.

oil companies, as if we are all out to destroy nature. People don't realize that in the past forty years the global environmentalist movement has changed the way we do things. We are monitored and held accountable for the slightest slip—but the squatters and 'cattle farmers' disappear the second they get into trouble. These criminals invade the jungle, poach animals, and cut down the big valuable trees. They sell them for practically nothing, then dump gasoline and torch the land until nothing is left! Once the grasses grow back they let loose a few cows on the 'pastureland.' It's a shrewd business strategy, but absolutely soulless—they don't have to face the consequences! If they keep this up, the only virgin jungles left will be protected national parks and Amazonian oilfields."

"Oilfields?" I ask.

"An operating company can get in big trouble for not following environmental protocols to the letter," José says. "Before developing, the Ministry of the Environment requires that we do a series of environmental and social impact studies, including remediation plans for after the work is done. We have to consider flora, fauna, communities, water, air, soil, and a host of other factors—in the wet *and* dry seasons to ensure we don't miss a single migratory animal or seasonal issue. In drilling, we have to identify the plants that will be displaced, and we are not allowed to cut down any large trees without special permission. Not all companies are exemplary—but most try to be. Times have changed since the 'wild west' days when oil companies weren't accountable for any destruction or contamination they caused.

We continue driving in companionable silence.

I look out the window with different eyes now: these pasturelands are actually a postapocalyptic Amazonia. It leaves me feeling cold, struggling through the complexity of the situation. I wish the entire Amazon could be protected, but I know this is unrealistic. People need to be given a way out of poverty, and a chance to improve their lives. Economic growth is a major political agenda for Peru right now, and an ever-growing international demand for agricultural products and raw materials are seen as important keys to participating in international trade (an impression reinforced by multinationals hungry for new and affordable suppliers). To meet this demand, the government encourages development in parts of the Amazon through titles and permits. However, not all development is done responsibly and in general, small scale local development is not monitored. This is especially true in high-poverty areas—care for the environment is often not considered.

I wrestle with the tremendous complexity of the problem before me—the Amazon is a varied land, roughly the size of 90 percent of the United States. The second you generalize it, the second you can be proven wrong. Different regions face different circumstances. There are also the historical factors to consider: the Conquest and European disease are thought to have wiped out between 80 to 90 percent of indigenous Amazonians. Survivors had to face "*los caucheros*" (the rubber barons)—whose atrocities make the Conquest look pleasant in comparison. Maybe the pasturelands out my window, are not the only scene of a postapocalyptic Amazonia. The past doesn't justify present environmental abuses, but it does help put the situation into context. Amazonians (whether living tradition-ally, in isolation or in modern society), non-Amazonians, and the whole spectrum between each have their own relationship with the jungle and with the modern, globalized world. In spite of the complexity, there is one premise that everyone shares: the jungle holds value—be it monetary, ecologic, or for tradi-tional survival, it is worth *something*.

To preserve the land in the long term, it's clear that the Amazon needs carefully planned conservation models that allow local people to profit from the eco-sensitive development of the land. Peruvian and international organizations are working hard to protect the virgin jungles—but looking out at the cleared fields all I can think is: how can we protect what is left of the jungle here? How can we bring back the jungle that we've lost? *These* are the frontlines of deforestation—jungle open for development, easily accessed by roads and nearby population centers.

A Shipibo shaman once told me, "The greatest threat to the jungle are the 'natives who have forgotten that they are natives—the ones who have forgotten the traditional respect of the jungle, and who use it for their own selfish reasons.'" This Shipibo shaman is a very well respected member of his community, and a vessel for Shipibo culture and traditional knowledge. When he said these words to me he was in full "western dress": modern glasses, a button-down collared shirt over a tank-top undershirt, neatly ironed black pants, and elegant leather shoes. Physically, he was indistinguishable from any modern Peruvian with indigenous heritage in Lima. Seeing such a powerful Amazonian figure in full western dress and wielding such an unexpected message taught me something important. We cannot go into Amazonian conservation with preconceived notions of all Amazonians living in harmony with the forest, wearing traditional clothing, and the clichéd "good" and "bad" guys of conservation. Yes, the past is deplorable: Amazonians *were* devastated by European diseases, the rubber barons *did* commit unspeakable atrocities, and traditional social structures *were* turned on their heads by the spread of globalization—but the Amazonian man who stood before me was *not* a shriveled victim of his circumstances, but a master survivor, and a vessel of his culture. His proud people masterfully adapted to life in the trying conditions of the jungle, where they learned to master plants for healing or harming in ways that rival the most advanced pharmaceutical labs. (Just read the work of Dr. Mark Plotkin or Dr. Wade Davis for more on this.)

The Amazonians survived the Inca, the Spanish, and the rubber barons—and they are now masterfully adapting to modernity. Redefining themselves in a blend of the traditional and the modern to not only survive, but thrive. What's more, sitting with the Shipibo shaman made something very clear—there is no difference between him and me. "His" people and "mine." We are all just trying to survive and be happy; we all want to be loved and successful, and we all have hopes and dreams. We are *all* natives of planet earth. How we choose to live in our own "jungles" is our own personal decision—but we cannot pretend our decisions don't have an environmental impact.

José's words give me hope—maybe responsible development can turn the tide. Maestro and others at Mayantuyacu had mentioned that Maple was a "good neighbor." Maybe oil and gas companies *can* become champions for the jungle, and maybe we *can* find a way for economic prosperity and environmental stewardship to go hand in hand. The give and take of adapting to new paradigms, the delicate balance of traditional and modern, the perplexing idea of "natives who forget they are natives," and the unexpected turn that oil companies can, under the right circumstances, serve as protectors of the jungle—they are far more complex than I had imagined. I feel there must be a solution in which the locals and oil companies can coexist with the good of the jungle as everyone's top concern. There is a solution hidden in these details—but for now it eludes me.

José's voice interrupts my thoughts, "There is the Agua Caliente

Dome!" He says pointing to a large, broad landform rising out of the jungle before us. From this distance the stark contrast between the deforested areas and the Dome's virgin jungle is clearly visible.

"Most of the land around us has been cleared, so our jungle has become an oasis for wildlife in the area. We are constantly on guard for poachers, loggers, and especially the clear-burners—we have gas lines in the area." José says.

"I really love this jungle," he continues. "I've worked here for years and it's helped me educate my kids and put food on the table. It breaks my heart to see it disappearing. They'll soon deforest the entire jungle around the oilfield. I am afraid of what will happen when the oilfield is no longer profitable and the investors decide to pull out. Our jungle won't last long."

Lush, beautiful forest suddenly dominates the roadside. We are entering Maple's jungle. Soon we reach the Agua Caliente oilfield at the top of the dome. The handful of large wooden buildings that make up the camp are in the midcentury "Equatorial Americana" outpost style. Everything is clean, neat, and well maintained. Large painted signs remind workers to properly dispose of waste, protect the environment, and not disturb the wildlife. Every newcomer undergoes a thorough training day on safety and environmental responsibility in the jungle, and I am no exception.

My fieldwork advances well, and by the end of the week I have the samples and measurements I need for my analyses. There is one thing left to do before I leave: visit Maestro. Since Maple Gas and Mayantuyacu both seek to protect the jungle from the clear-burners, I take José with me.

Getting to Mayantuyacu from the oilfield is difficult. There are no roads and the most direct path is through the jungle. Though it's only about a mile from the northernmost well site, the terrain is rough and, to my delight, filled with virgin jungle. After an arduous two-hour hike through thick, pristine jungle, dense leaf litter, and rugged topography, we arrive at Mayantuyacu in a heavy rain. As always, I scan the cliff for the sign that I've arrived: the guardian tree, the huge twisting Came Renaco. To my horror, I see through the pelting rain that Mayantuyacu's iconic tree has broken in half. Its upper half is still partially attached to the trunk, but the great tree's Gorgon head lies helpless in the surge of the river. I know what this must mean to Mayantuyacu—to Maestro.

I leave José in the maloca and run to Maestro's house to find him curled up in his hammock. He looks up in surprise. "Andrés!" he says. He rises slowly from the hammock and greets me with a frail embrace. He does not look well.

I ask, "Are you okay?"

"You saw the Came Renaco?" he asks. He looks forlorn. "We all get old. I'm sad and a bit sick. But I don't mind being sick—it teaches me I still have more to learn. Tell me now, how did you get here?"

I explain everything—the Moran Papers, the fieldwork with Maple, the trek through the jungle. With a bit of apprehension, I ask Maestro if he would be willing to meet with Maple's geologist. Without hesitation, he agrees. "Maple is a good neighbor—we both keep to ourselves and don't bother each other. Bring him."

We sit together on Maestro's terrace as I make the introductions. Soon, he and José are sharing their love of the jungle, and their concern about the threats that face it.

"Maple won't be in this area forever," José tells Maestro. "Eventually the oil will run out, and I greatly fear for the jungle after we leave. If you haven't considered getting this place legally protected, I highly suggest you start looking into it. I know Andrés is helping you with a conservation plan, and the work he is doing to document the river will be essential. There is also a Ministry of the Environment office in Pucallpa that might help."

Maestro listens stoically and nods after José finishes speaking. He knows what needs to be done.

An hour later, José and I start on the path to the Pachitea River, where Francisco Pizarro will take us by boat to Maple's dock. The rain has stopped, and we set a quick pace down the familiar trail through jungle I have come to know well.

Halfway to the Pachitea, an unfamiliar sight stops me dead in my tracks: a large patch of jungle—gone. All that remains of the massive, awe-inspiring trees are piles of sawdust and wood chips around huge stumps.

I stand silently at the edge of the clearing, looking out at the ruin before me. In less than a year, a large part of the Boiling River's jungle has disappeared.

José inspects the scene. Anger and sadness welling in his voice, he says, "There must have been a number of good lumber trees here. If not, all this would have been burned off already. I'm sure that is coming next."

Thermal cameras present the safest, fastest, and most reliable way to take temperature measurements at the Boiling River.

14 Paititi

It's May 2014, the evening of my first day back at Mayantuyacu. I sit under the maloca's electric lights, preparing for my fieldwork. My laptop charges to the sputtering sounds of Mayantuyacu's electric generator. Maestro says the spirits don't like the noise.

I have no doubt that one day Mayantuyacu will offer twenty-four-hour electricity, phone lines, and Internet access. These things will make life easier, more efficient, and more comfortable for the community, and also greatly help the monitoring and conservation efforts to protect the area. Still I can't help feeling a little apprehensive about how this will change life here.

The nine months since my last visit have brought drastic changes—the very changes that José predicted. The jungle is disappearing.

Thanks to Google's support I now have high-resolution satellite imagery of the area around the Boiling River. A colleague from Google warned me that the images weren't recent, and that deforestation had likely advanced significantly since they were taken. He was absolutely right.

These images, from 2004, 2005, 2010, and 2011, show a sobering reality: clear-burnings, pastureland, and deforestation spreading with each passing year. They still didn't prepare me for this 2014 journey into the jungle. Nine months ago the trip from Pucallpa to Mayantuyacu required a two-hour drive, a thirty-minute *pekepeke* ride, and an hour-long walk through the jungle. This year, deforestation made the trip a comfortable three-hour drive. The jungle along the way has been replaced by pastureland, dotted with the charred remains of large trees and a few grazing cows.

It's painful to compare the satellite images to an aerial photograph from the 1940s, when the area was almost entirely covered by jungle. Still, I can't help but notice that the area controlled by the oil company has remained virtually unchanged, despite heavy development.

Development is coming—but it does not have to mean destruction. Done responsibly and consciously, development can protect the area rather than raze it. At my side are my empty sample bottles, and the notebook that will be filled with the week's fieldwork. Documenting the details of what makes this incredible geothermal system so unique is the key to ensuring its future. With each new data point, I am working to show the world why this place is such a marvel, why it deserves to be protected—and to ensure that whoever controls this area understands the Boiling River's significance. Fortunately I am not alone in this endeavor. Mayantuyacu's "tribe" extends far beyond this jungle, and includes countless foreigners from all over the world who have visited this incredible place, and who care for it as much as I do. The river has brought us all together. A Canadian group is working with the locals to help Mayantuyacu minimize its environmental footprint. Italians are also collaborating with Mayantuyacu to identify the healing properties of

Geochemical water sampling at La Bomba. This bubbling, churning part of the river boasts temperatures around 97°C (207°F). Though steamer's gloves temporarily protect my hands from the intense temperatures, I stay low to the ground, both to avoid the scalding steam and to stabilize myself against falling.

the plant medicines as Americans collaborate on to study the anthropological significance of the place. I am continuing my studies and am bringing together Peruvians from the jungle and the cities in order to obtain legal protection for the Boiling River.

I keep working until the generator goes silent and the lights slowly flicker off.

Full of conviction and excited to start my fieldwork tomorrow, I walk back to my hut in the darkness. As my eyes adjust to the starlit night, I am amazed at this world that moments before had appeared only as a black void beyond the electric lights.

The week passes quickly. Each day, I collect samples of water, rock, and minerals. I plan to analyze them back in the lab, hoping to better understand the relationship between the waters and the rock formations they flow through. This year, for the first time, I am also studying the extremophile life-forms—algae, bacteria, and other microorganisms—that live in and around the Boiling River at temperatures that would kill most life-forms.

On the eve of my departure from Mayantuyacu, I walk out of my hut into the cool evening air. It is time to say good-bye.

Maestro lies comfortably in his hammock while Luis, our old jungle guide, sits on a floor cushion and puffs away at a *mapacho*. Mauro, Maestro's new apprentice, sits on a low plastic stool. "*Buenas noches*," I call.

"The young doctor!" Maestro smiles, his eyes glimmering through the smoke.

"We have barely seen you this past week," says Mauro.

"I've been working," I respond.

"It's true," Luis says. "I saw him many times, always alone with the river." Then, turning to me: "You move through the jungle differently now."

I am surprised. "When did you see me? I thought I was alone the entire time!" Luis smiles mischievously.

"It's true—he moves differently now," Maestro says. "How are your studies going?" he asks me.

I fill him in on my research. He listens attentively, eager to understand how the Great Civilization shows significance through measurements. I relay how identifying the processes and mechanisms that create the river will identify the sensitive areas—both above- and underground—that will require the most protection, and reassure him that together we, Amazonians and non-Amazonians, will find a way to respect the spirits and protect the jungle.

"Maestro," I say. "Since my first visit I've been impressed with how well-known Mayantuyacu is among foreigners, while being virtually unknown in Peru—how did this happen?"

He smiles through curling eddies of smoke from his *mapacho*. "At first I wanted this place only for Amazonians—to preserve our culture and our jungle. But people have been seduced by the Great Civilization. Our young only want to be in Lima, and our old have forgotten how to treat the jungle. I didn't know what to do, so I asked the plants, and I had a vision."

He pauses and looks hard at me. "Remember when you came the second time, you had a sinus problem and I gave you a medicine?"

"Of course—Ishpingo. It worked great."

"Ishpingo is a large tree, with a very powerful spirit. In my vision I was sitting under a great Ishpingo when the Ishpingo Spirit appeared to me in the form of a tall, thin white man, dressed in all white, with a long, white beard. Everything about the man shone bright white. When I asked the spirit why it had taken that form, it replied that the salvation of this jungle would come with foreigners. The next day, I took my first foreign patient and now I have foreign apprentices. The Ishpingo Spirit was right: the world has changed, and we need to learn from each other—the ancient ways, and the ways of the Great Civilization."

This jungle is a place of legends and visions, I think.

All at once, another detail from my grandfather's legend surfaces—a detail I'd wanted to ask Maestro about for years. The time had just never seemed right, or perhaps I'd always feared seeming foolish. But now, sitting beside him, having discovered that legends can be true, I finally summon the nerve.

"Maestro," I say, "does Paititi, the city of gold, actually exist?"

Maestro raises his brows in surprise. "You mean you've missed it?"

I look at him, confused.

Maestro laughs, then gestures to the jungle all around us.

Suddenly I understand. When the conquistadors had asked about Paititi, the Inca did not lie. For the Inca, gold was a symbol of life itself. A city of gold is therefore, a city of life—and where is there more life than in the Amazon? Inca vengeance came with a play on words, the significance of which the conquistadors could never understand.

I laugh, and shake my head in wonder. This jungle, this river, is more than just a place to be protected. It's proof that the world is still so full of mystery, and that for all our knowledge, nature will always be a few steps ahead of us.

The light from my headlamp cuts through the darkness as I walk back to my hut. Passing the Came Renaco's stump, I stop and turn to the stone steps leading down to the river. I descend to the rocky shore below, engulfed by vapor. Slowly, carefully, I find my way onto a large rock in the middle of the churning waters.

All around, the jungle pulses with the sounds of life: croaking frogs, chirping insects, rustling canopies, the intergalactic sounds of passing bats. At the center is the booming, surging river. Eddies of rising vapor dance through the cool night air to join the innumerable stars of the Milky Way.

I wonder how long we have before the lights of civilization invade this part of the Amazon. Will my work bring them here faster? What are my responsibilities to science? To the people who live here? To the sacred river? Maestro once said, "we conceal to protect"—but now we are doing the opposite. I think of explorers whose discoveries threatened to destroy the things they discovered. Here in Peru, when Hiram Bingham first saw Machu Picchu, did he imagine the impact he would have on the country's culture, its economy, its place in the world's imagination? Did he ever spend a night sitting alone among the ruins, wondering, *How can we preserve this place if we reveal it to the world?* My instincts tell me that the path to preservation lies in showing the world that they need to protect this stunning natural phenomenon. But what if I'm wrong?

Standing on the rock, I realize that studying the river has taught me far more about myself than about geology, geothermal features, or native cultures. As Maestro said, "the river shows us what we need to see." A friend once asked why I keep coming back to this place. I realize now that it's because here you are forced to be intentional, to face your own limits and work within them. Every step must be measured. Mistakes have painful consequences. You can't afford distractions.

My headlamp concentrates my focus on the small area it illuminates and makes the darkness beyond seem impenetrable. I contemplate the marvels that must be out there, shrouded in darkness or hidden in the everyday. That is the lesson of the darkness: it is our perspective that draws the line between the known and the unknown, the sacred and the trivial, the things we take for granted and the things we have yet to discover.

I had missed the darkness.

EPILOGUE

Sometimes I'll pick up the "heart of the jungle" fossil on my bookshelf, or pull out my field notebooks from my desk drawer, warped by Amazonian rains and the river's steam, the scent of the jungle still on their pages. I do this to remind myself that fiction does not have a monopoly on the unbelievable. If it wasn't for the data, photos, videos, and other evidence I've collected over the past few years, I sometimes feel that I might mistake my entire experience with the river for a dream.

It is July 2015, and the river is not yet legally protected. It does not appear as a significant site on any map. If we are successful, all this will change, and Peru will have a "new" wonder.

I could have begun publishing about the river in 2011, in scientific journals or in the mainstream media. Instead, I have kept the overwhelming majority of my work in the dark. I am working closely with Maestro and Sandra as well as with Peruvian and international conservation groups to introduce the river to the world responsibly.

Our goal is responsible development that empowers and benefits those who live in the area. Unveiling the river without preparing the locals would have risked uncontrolled development and irresponsible tourism. It could have done more harm than good.

I am working with Mayantuyacu and Santuario Huishtín (another Amazonian healing center on the Boiling River run by a former apprentice of Maestro), presenting them with information that enables them to determine the best future for their communities. Mayantuyacu is working to expand its ecotourism operations, to minimize its environmental impact on the jungle, and to create an educational center for Asháninka culture and traditional medicine. Maestro's vision of the Ishpingo appears to be coming true: Mayantuyacu's "tribe" has grown to include people from all over the world who are working to protect it.

Next month I'll be back in the jungle, collecting the final samples and ending my five-year study of the Boiling River. Though the work is not finished, the preliminary results reveal that the world is, in fact, more amazing than I had ever imagined. Working with Dr. Jonathan Eisen, a microbiologist from UC Davis, and Dr. Spencer Wells, a geneticist from the National Geographic Society, among others, our team has identified previously undocumented species of extremophile microorganisms living in and around the Boiling River at temperatures that would kill us. Understanding how these microorganisms thrive in such extreme conditions, and seeing how they compare to other extremophiles in geothermal systems across the globe, could ideally help shed light on the mystery of where life on our planet came from.

I've also found other thermal rivers in the Peruvian Amazon—though none remotely comparable in size and volume to the Boiling River. The scientific and conservation efforts surrounding this complex system are too detailed to summarize here, so to learn more, or to directly support the scientific and conservation work, please visit boilingriver.org (with a Spanish version at riohirviente.org), where the scientific data and other information are fully available for those interested in learning more about this great natural wonder. There is so much hidden in our world, occulted in the everyday—both in the unknown and in what we think we understand. Be curious. There is significance in the landscapes we pass by, in the pixels of Google Earth's satellite imagery, and in the smallest details in stories. Within the next year, this first phase of my research will be complete. The river will be put on the map, and I will finally step outside my lab and pour the water samples I've collected onto the ground, so that the waters, as Maestro once said, can find their way back home.

Heading back to Mayantuyacu after a long day of work in the jungle.

ACKNOWLEDGMENTS

With deepest gratitude, I want to thank those individuals and organizations whose love, support, and guidance have made this work possible.

My grandfather, Daniel Ruzo, the greatest storyteller I know. My aunt Guida and uncle Eo Gastelumendi—and their dinner parties. My parents, Andrés and Ana, my uncle Octavio, my godfather Javier, and the amazing group of people that I am blessed to call my family.

Thanks to the Boiling River, its jungle, and those who watch over it and have given me the honor of sharing your wonder with the world; in particular to Maestro Juan, Sandra, Luis, Mauro, Brunswick, and the whole Mayantuyacu community; as well as, Maestro Enrique and the Santuario Huishtín community, and Maple Gas, particularly José Carlos.

To TED—your talks have changed my life, and I'm honored to be part of your mission. Thank you to Kelly Stoetzel, Rives, Bruno Giussani, Chris Anderson, Ellyn Guttman, Alex Hofmann and the entire TED family.

Special thanks to my editor, Michelle Quint. Your hard work, patience, and dedication helped an idea become a book worth spreading. Thank you.

Thanks to the SMU community: Maria Richards, David Blackwell, Andrew Quicksall, Drew Aleto, Jumana Haj Abed, Al Walbel, Kurt Ferguson, Roy Beavers, Robert Gregory and my PhD Committee. Also to Jim and Carole Young, and Sharon and Bobby Lyle—who first introduced me to TED Talks.

Also thanks to Alfonso Callejas, Carlos Espinosa, Peter Koutsogeorgas, Basil Koutsogeorgas, Whitney Olson, José Fajri, and Devlin Gundy. Shannon K. McCall, his family, and the Telios Corporation. Google, particularly Charles Baron and Christiaan Adams. The Geothermal Resources Council. William E. Gipson and the AAPG. Jose and Felipe Koechlin, Mark Plotkin, the Sociedad Peruana de Derecho Ambiental, UC Santa Barbara, the Moran Trust, INGEMMET, PeruPetro, Donald Thomas, Jonathan Eisen, and Spencer Wells. To my colleagues at the National Geographic Society, particularly Emily Landis, Chris Thornton, and Wade Davis. As well as National Geographic Learning, the schools who use these materials and have helped fund my research, and the kids who learn from them, and inspire me to protect our amazing world.

Lastly, and most importantly, I want to thank my wife, Sofía. I could not have done this without you. You are my rock—and as a geologist you know how much that means to me.

IMAGE CREDITS

ABOUT THE AUTHOR

Andrés Ruzo grew up in the United States, Nicaragua, and Peru. Besides giving him a bit of a national identity crisis, his background helped him see that the world's problems are not confined by borders, but rather share a common root in energy and resources. This realization inspired him to become a geothermal scientist: obtaining degrees in Geology and Finance at Southern Methodist University, where he is currently finishing his PhD in Geophysics. He believes that environmental responsibility and economic prosperity can go hand in hand, and uses science to unite both aims. He is a National Geographic Explorer, an avid science communicator, and a passionate developer of educational content.

A percentage of the proceeds from this TED Book will serve to fund scientific and conservation work at the Boiling River.

For more information, on the Boiling River or how you can help support the scientific and conservation work done to protect it, please visit boilingriver.org.

WATCH ANDRÉS RUZO'S TED TALK

Andrés Ruzo's TED Talk, available for free at TED.com, is the companion to *The Boiling River*.

PHOTO: JAMES DUNCAN DAVIDSON/TED

Mark Plotkin
What the People of the Amazon Know That You Don't

"The greatest and most endangered species in the Amazon rainforest is not the jaguar or the harpy eagle," says Mark Plotkin, "It's the isolated and uncontacted tribes." In an energetic and sobering talk, the ethnobotanist brings us into the world of the forest's indigenous tribes and the incredible medicinal plants that their shamans use to heal. He outlines the challenges and perils that are endangering them—and their wisdom—and urges us to protect this irreplaceable repository of knowledge.

Nathan Wolfe
What's Left to Explore

We've been to the moon, we've mapped the continents, we've even been to the deepest point in the ocean—twice. What's left for the next generation to explore? Biologist and explorer Nathan Wolfe suggests this answer: "Almost everything. And we can start," he says, "with the world of the unseeably small."

Antonio Donato Nobre
The Magic of the Amazon: A River That Flows Invisibly All Around Us

The Amazon River is like a heart, pumping water from the seas through it, and up into the atmosphere through 600 billion trees, which act like lungs. Clouds form, rain falls, and the forest thrives. In a lyrical talk, Antonio Donato Nobre talks us through the interconnected systems of this region, and how they provide environmental services to the entire world. A parable for the extraordinary symphony that is nature.

Louie Schwartzberg
Hidden Miracles of the Natural World

We live in a world of unseeable beauty, so subtle and delicate that it is imperceptible to the human eye. To bring this invisible world to light, filmmaker Louie Schwartzberg bends the boundaries of time and space with high-speed cameras, time lapses, and microscopes. At TED2014, he shares highlights from his latest project, a 3D film titled *Mysteries of the Unseen World*, which slows down, speeds up, and magnifies the astonishing wonders of nature.

The Laws of Medicine
Field Notes from an Uncertain Science
by Siddhartha Mukherjee

Essential, required reading for doctors and patients alike: A Pulitzer Prize–winning author and one of the world's premiere cancer researchers reveals an urgent philosophy on the little-known principles that govern medicine—and how understanding these principles can empower us all.

The Art of Stillness
Adventures in Going Nowhere
by Pico Iyer

In a world beset by the distractions and demands of technology, acclaimed travel writer Pico Iyer reflects on why so many of us are desperate to unplug and bring stillness into our lives.

Follow Your Gut
The Enormous Impact of Tiny Microbes
by Rob Knight with Brendan Buhler

In this groundbreaking book, scientist Rob Knight reveals how the microscopic life within our bodies—particularly within our intestines—has an astonishing impact on our lives. Your health, mood, sleep patterns, eating preferences, and more can all be traced in part to the tiny creatures that live on and inside of us.

ABOUT TED BOOKS

TED Books are small books about big ideas. They're short enough to read in a single sitting, but long enough to delve deep into a topic. The wide-ranging series covers everything from architecture to business, space travel to love, and is perfect for anyone with a curious mind and an expansive love of learning.

Each TED Book is paired with a related TED Talk, available online at TED.com. The books pick up where the talks leave off. An 18-minute speech can plant a seed or spark the imagination, but many talks create a need to go deeper, to learn more, to tell a longer story. TED Books fill this need.

ABOUT TED

TED is a nonprofit devoted to spreading ideas, usually in the form of short, powerful talks (eighteen minutes or less) but also through books, animation, radio programs, and events. TED began in 1984 as a conference where Technology, Entertainment, and Design converged, and today it covers almost every topic—from science to business to global issues—in more than one hundred languages.

TED is a global community, welcoming people from every discipline and culture who seek a deeper understanding of the world. We believe passionately in the power of ideas to change attitudes, lives, and, ultimately, our future. On TED .com, we're building a clearinghouse of free knowledge from the world's most inspired thinkers—and a community of curious souls to engage with ideas and each other. Our annual flagship conference convenes thought leaders from all fields to exchange ideas.

Our TEDx program allows communities worldwide to host their own independent, local events all year long. And our Open Translation Project ensures these ideas can move across borders.

In fact, everything we do—from the TED Radio Hour to the projects sparked by the TED Prize, from TEDx events to the TED-Ed lesson series—is driven by this goal: How can we best spread great ideas?

TED is owned by a nonprofit, nonpartisan foundation.